Table Of Contents

Triumphs and Consequences: Things Not Known about the Founding Fathers—Architects of America

1.1 The Birth of a Nation

The birth of the United States of America was a momentous event in world history. It marked the beginning of a new era, where a group of visionary individuals came together to create a nation founded on principles of liberty, equality, and self-governance. These individuals, known as the Founding Fathers, played a crucial role in shaping the destiny of the nation and laying the foundation for its future success.

The Founding Fathers were a diverse group of men who hailed from different backgrounds and regions of the country. They were lawyers, merchants, farmers, and intellectuals, united by a common desire to break free from British rule and establish a government that would protect the rights and freedoms of its citizens. Among the most prominent Founding Fathers were George Washington, Thomas Jefferson, John Adams, Benjamin Franklin, James Madison, and Alexander Hamilton.

The journey towards independence began with the American Revolution, a long and arduous struggle against the British Empire. The Founding Fathers played pivotal roles in leading the colonies to victory, both on the battlefield and in the realm of ideas. They rallied the American people, inspired them with their words, and fought for their rights and liberties. Through their leadership and determination, they were able to secure independence for the United States.

One of the most significant achievements of the Founding Fathers was the drafting of the Declaration of Independence. Authored primarily by Thomas Jefferson, this document proclaimed the colonies' separation from Britain and articulated the principles upon which the new nation would be built. It declared that all men are created equal and endowed with certain unalienable rights, including life, liberty, and the pursuit of happiness. The Declaration of Independence served as a rallying cry for the American people and laid the groundwork for the establishment of a democratic republic.

Following the successful conclusion of the Revolutionary War, the Founding Fathers turned their attention to the task of creating a new system of government. They recognized the need for a stronger central authority that could effectively govern the nation while still preserving individual liberties. This led to the drafting of the United States Constitution, a remarkable document that remains the supreme law of the land to this day.

The Founding Fathers, often referred to as the "Architects of the Constitution," engaged in intense debates and negotiations to craft a framework that would balance power between the federal government and the states. They sought to establish a system of checks and balances that would prevent any one branch of government from becoming too powerful. The Constitution also enshrined the rights and freedoms of the American people, including the right to free speech, the right to bear arms, and the right to a fair trial.

However, the birth of the nation was not without its challenges and consequences. The Founding Fathers had to grapple with issues such as slavery, the treatment of Native Americans, and the role of women in society. These complex issues would continue to shape the nation's history and have lasting impacts on its development.

In conclusion, the birth of the United States of America was a remarkable achievement brought about by the vision, courage, and determination of the Founding Fathers. Through their leadership and intellect, they laid the foundation for a nation that would become a beacon of freedom and democracy. While they faced numerous challenges and their actions had consequences, their triumphs far outweighed their failures. The United States stands today as a testament to their enduring legacy and the enduring principles upon which it was founded.

1.2 The Architects of the Declaration of Independence

The Declaration of Independence is one of the most significant documents in American history. It not only declared the United States' independence from Great Britain but also laid the foundation for the principles and values that would shape the nation. Behind this monumental document were a group of extraordinary individuals known as the Founding Fathers, who played a crucial role in its creation. These architects of the Declaration of Independence were visionaries, philosophers, and statesmen who dedicated their lives to the cause of liberty and the establishment of a new nation.

Thomas Jefferson

Thomas Jefferson, the primary author of the Declaration of Independence, was a man of immense intellect and vision. Born in Virginia in 1743, Jefferson was well-educated and deeply influenced by Enlightenment thinkers such as John Locke and Jean-Jacques Rousseau. His belief in natural rights, including life, liberty, and the pursuit of happiness, formed the basis of the Declaration's famous opening lines.

Jefferson's eloquent words captured the spirit of the American Revolution and articulated the grievances of the colonists against British rule. His skillful writing and persuasive arguments made the Declaration a powerful statement of independence and a rallying cry for the American people.

John Adams

John Adams, a Massachusetts lawyer and diplomat, played a crucial role in the drafting and adoption of the Declaration of Independence. Adams was a passionate advocate for independence and tirelessly worked to build support for the cause. His influence and persuasive abilities were instrumental in convincing the Continental Congress to declare independence from Britain.

Adams also served on the committee responsible for drafting the Declaration, and while he did not write the document himself, his contributions were significant. He provided valuable insights and helped shape the final version of the Declaration, ensuring that it reflected the ideals and aspirations of the American people.

Benjamin Franklin

Benjamin Franklin, a polymath and one of the most renowned figures of the American Revolution, also played a vital role in the creation of the Declaration of Independence. Franklin's wisdom, diplomacy, and scientific acumen made him a respected figure both in America and abroad.

As a member of the Continental Congress, Franklin was involved in the editing and revision of the Declaration. His experience and reputation lent credibility to the document and helped garner support for its adoption. Franklin's diplomatic skills were also crucial in securing foreign alliances, particularly with France, which proved instrumental in the American victory in the Revolutionary War.

Roger Sherman

Roger Sherman, a lawyer and statesman from Connecticut, was another key figure in the creation of the Declaration of Independence. Sherman was known for his practical approach and his ability to find common ground among differing opinions. He played a significant role in the Continental Congress and served on the committee responsible for drafting the Declaration.

Sherman's contributions to the document were primarily in the form of edits and revisions. He helped refine the language and structure of the Declaration, ensuring that it accurately conveyed the grievances and aspirations of the American people. Sherman's commitment to compromise and his dedication to the cause of independence made him an invaluable member of the committee.

Robert Livingston

Robert Livingston, a prominent New York lawyer and statesman, was also involved in the creation of the Declaration of Independence. Livingston's legal expertise and political acumen made him a valuable asset in the Continental Congress.

While Livingston did not serve on the committee responsible for drafting the Declaration, he played a crucial role in its adoption. As a member of the New York delegation, Livingston voted in favor of independence and signed the document on behalf of his state. His support and commitment to the cause of liberty were essential in securing unanimous approval for the Declaration.

Conclusion

The architects of the Declaration of Independence were remarkable individuals who possessed the courage, intellect, and vision to create a new nation. Through their collective efforts, they crafted a document that not only declared independence but also laid the groundwork for a democratic society based on the principles of liberty, equality, and justice.

The contributions of Thomas Jefferson, John Adams, Benjamin Franklin, Roger Sherman, and Robert Livingston were instrumental in shaping the Declaration and ensuring its adoption. Their tireless dedication to the cause of independence and their unwavering belief in the rights of the American people continue to inspire generations.

The Declaration of Independence stands as a testament to the enduring legacy of these Founding Fathers. Their triumphs and consequences, their victories and challenges, have left an indelible mark on the history of the United States, making them true architects of America.

1.3 The Builders of the Constitution

The Founding Fathers of the United States were not only the architects of the Declaration of Independence but also the builders of the Constitution. After declaring independence from British rule, the newly formed nation faced the daunting task of creating a framework for governance that would ensure the rights and liberties of its citizens while establishing a strong and effective central government. This section explores the challenges, debates, compromises, and triumphs that characterized the process of building the Constitution.

The Need for a New Constitution

Following the American Revolution, the United States operated under the Articles of Confederation, a loose alliance of states that lacked a strong central government. The weaknesses of this system soon became apparent, as the country struggled with issues such as economic instability, interstate disputes, and the inability to effectively address national concerns. It became clear that a new constitution was necessary to establish a more unified and efficient government.

The Constitutional Convention

In May 1787, delegates from twelve of the thirteen states (Rhode Island abstained) gathered in Philadelphia for the Constitutional Convention. The purpose of the convention was to revise the Articles of Confederation, but it quickly became apparent that a complete overhaul was needed. The delegates, including notable figures such as George Washington, James Madison, and Benjamin Franklin, embarked on the monumental task of drafting a new constitution.

Debates and Compromises

The process of building the Constitution was not without its challenges. The delegates held differing views on issues such as representation, the powers of the central government, and the balance of power between the states and the federal government. These debates often led to heated discussions and impassioned arguments.

One of the most contentious issues was the question of representation in the legislative branch. Larger states favored a system based on population, while smaller states feared being overshadowed and advocated for equal representation. The Great Compromise, proposed by Roger Sherman, resolved this issue by creating a bicameral legislature with a House of Representatives based on population and a Senate with equal representation for each state.

Another significant debate centered around the institution of slavery. Southern states, heavily reliant on slave labor, sought to protect their interests, while Northern states pushed for the abolition of slavery. The Three-Fifths Compromise was reached, counting each enslaved person as three-fifths of a person for the purposes of representation and taxation.

Ratification and the Bill of Rights

Once the Constitution was drafted, it faced the challenge of ratification. The document required approval from at least nine of the thirteen states to become law. This process sparked intense debates and public discussions across the country.

Supporters of the Constitution, known as Federalists, argued for its ratification, emphasizing the need for a strong central government to ensure stability and protect the rights of citizens. Anti-Federalists, on the other hand, expressed concerns about the potential for government overreach and the lack of explicit protections for individual liberties.

To address these concerns, the Federalists agreed to add a Bill of Rights to the Constitution. These ten amendments, which guaranteed fundamental rights such as freedom of speech, religion, and the right to a fair trial, helped secure the support of many Anti-Federalists and ultimately led to the ratification of the Constitution.

The Birth of the American Presidency

One of the most significant achievements of the Constitutional Convention was the establishment of the American presidency. The delegates recognized the need for a strong executive branch to lead the nation and ensure the enforcement of laws. They debated the powers and limitations of the presidency, ultimately settling on a system that balanced authority with checks and balances.

The Constitution outlined the qualifications, powers, and responsibilities of the president, including the ability to veto legislation, serve as commander-in-chief of the military, and appoint key government officials. The delegates also established a system of electoral college to select the president, striking a compromise between direct popular vote and congressional appointment.

The Legacy of the Constitution

The Constitution, as built by the Founding Fathers, has endured for over two centuries and remains the supreme law of the land in the United States. Its creation marked a pivotal moment in history, as it established a framework for democratic governance that has served as a model for nations around the world.

The builders of the Constitution, through their debates, compromises, and vision, created a system of government that has allowed the United States to adapt and grow while preserving the fundamental principles of liberty, justice, and equality. The Constitution continues to be interpreted and applied by the judicial branch, ensuring that it remains a living document that can evolve with the changing needs of society.

In popular culture, the Founding Fathers and the Constitution have become symbols of American democracy and freedom. Their names and faces adorn monuments, currency, and countless historical works. However, it is important to recognize that they were not infallible and that their decisions had both triumphs and consequences. The Constitution, while a remarkable achievement, also contained compromises that perpetuated injustices such as slavery and limited the rights of certain groups.

In conclusion, the builders of the Constitution were faced with the immense task of creating a framework for a new nation. Through debates, compromises, and the inclusion of a Bill of Rights, they crafted a document that has stood the test of time. The Constitution remains a testament to the vision and foresight of the Founding Fathers, while also serving as a reminder of the ongoing work needed to ensure a more perfect union.

1.4 The Visionaries of a New Nation

The Founding Fathers of the United States were not only architects and builders of a new nation, but they were also visionaries who had a clear vision of what they wanted America to become. They were driven by a desire for freedom, equality, and the pursuit of happiness. In this section, we will explore the visionary ideas and principles that guided the Founding Fathers in shaping the future of the nation.

The Vision of Freedom

One of the central visions of the Founding Fathers was the idea of freedom. They believed in the inherent rights of individuals to live free from tyranny and oppression. This vision was reflected in the Declaration of Independence, where Thomas Jefferson wrote, "We hold these truths to be self-evident, that all men are created equal, that they are endowed by their Creator with certain unalienable Rights, that among these are Life, Liberty and the pursuit of Happiness."

The Founding Fathers understood that true freedom required a government that protected the rights of its citizens. They envisioned a system of government that would be based on the consent of the governed, where the power would be derived from the people themselves. This vision led to the creation of a democratic republic, where the people would elect representatives to make decisions on their behalf.

The Vision of Equality

In addition to freedom, the Founding Fathers also had a vision of equality. They believed that all individuals, regardless of their background or social status, should have equal opportunities and rights. This vision was enshrined in the Constitution, which guaranteed equal protection under the law and prohibited discrimination based on race, religion, or gender.

However, it is important to note that the Founding Fathers' vision of equality was not without its limitations. Slavery, for example, was a glaring contradiction to their vision of equality. Many of the Founding Fathers themselves were slaveholders, and it would take many years of struggle and sacrifice before the nation would fully confront the issue of slavery and work towards achieving true equality for all.

The Vision of Progress

The Founding Fathers were also visionaries in terms of progress and the advancement of society. They believed in the power of education, innovation, and scientific progress to improve the lives of individuals and society as a whole. They understood that a well-educated and informed citizenry was essential for the success of a democratic republic.

To promote progress, the Founding Fathers established institutions such as libraries, universities, and scientific societies. They also encouraged the pursuit of knowledge and the exchange of ideas. Benjamin Franklin, for example, was not only a statesman but also a renowned scientist and inventor who made significant contributions to various fields.

The Vision of Unity

Another important vision of the Founding Fathers was the idea of unity. They recognized the importance of a united nation in order to achieve their goals and protect the rights and freedoms of its citizens. This vision was evident in the creation of a strong federal government with powers that were carefully balanced between the national and state levels.

The Founding Fathers also emphasized the need for compromise and cooperation among the states. They understood that a diverse nation with different interests and perspectives would require a system that allowed for the peaceful resolution of conflicts. This vision of unity and cooperation laid the foundation for the success of the American experiment.

The Vision of a Lasting Legacy

Above all, the Founding Fathers had a vision of creating a lasting legacy for future generations. They understood that the decisions they made and the principles they established would shape the nation for years to come. They believed in the importance of preserving their ideas and values, which is why they left behind a wealth of writings and documents that continue to guide and inspire us today.

The visionaries of a new nation, the Founding Fathers, were driven by a deep sense of purpose and a commitment to creating a better future. Their visionary ideas of freedom, equality, progress, unity, and a lasting legacy continue to shape the United States of America. As we explore their triumphs and consequences, we gain a deeper understanding of the principles that have made America the greatest nation in history.

Triumphs and Challenges of the Revolutionary War

2.1 The Road to Revolution

The road to revolution was a tumultuous journey that ultimately led to the birth of a new nation. It was a period marked by intense political and social unrest, as the American colonies sought to break free from the grip of British rule. The seeds of revolution were sown long before the first shots were fired, as the colonists grappled with issues of taxation, representation, and individual rights.

The road to revolution can be traced back to the French and Indian War, which ended in 1763. This conflict, fought between the British and French, left Britain with a massive debt. In an effort to recoup their losses, the British government imposed a series of taxes on the American colonies. These included the Sugar Act of 1764, the Stamp Act of 1765, and the Townshend Acts of 1767. These measures were met with widespread resistance from the colonists, who believed that they were being unfairly taxed without representation in the British Parliament.

The colonists' opposition to British rule was further fueled by the writings of influential thinkers such as John Locke and Thomas Paine. Locke's ideas on natural rights and the social contract resonated with many colonists, who began to question the legitimacy of British authority. Paine's pamphlet, "Common Sense," published in 1776, argued for complete independence from Britain and became a rallying cry for the revolutionary cause.

The road to revolution reached a turning point with the Boston Massacre of 1770. Tensions between British soldiers and colonists had been escalating for some time, and on March 5th, a confrontation between a group of colonists and British troops resulted in the deaths of five colonists. This event further galvanized public opinion against British rule and fueled calls for independence.

The road to revolution continued to gain momentum with the Boston Tea Party of 1773. In response to the Tea Act, which granted a monopoly on tea sales to the British East India Company, a group of colonists disguised as Native Americans boarded British ships and dumped chests of tea into Boston Harbor. This act of defiance sent a clear message to the British government that the colonists were willing to take drastic measures to assert their rights.

The road to revolution culminated in the signing of the Declaration of Independence on July 4, 1776. This historic document, drafted primarily by Thomas Jefferson, proclaimed the colonies' independence from Britain and outlined the principles upon which the new nation would be founded. The signing of the Declaration of Independence marked the official beginning of the American Revolution.

The road to revolution was not without its challenges and sacrifices. The colonists faced a well-trained and well-equipped British army, and the odds seemed stacked against them. However, they were driven by a deep desire for freedom and a belief in the principles of liberty and self-governance. The Revolutionary War, which followed the signing of the Declaration of Independence, would test the resolve and determination of the American people.

The road to revolution had profound consequences for both the American colonies and the world at large. The successful rebellion against British rule inspired other nations to fight for their own independence and set a precedent for the establishment of democratic governments. The principles articulated in the Declaration of Independence, such as the belief in natural rights and the consent of the governed, continue to shape the political landscape of the United States to this day.

In conclusion, the road to revolution was a transformative period in American history. It was a time of great upheaval and uncertainty, but it was also a time of immense courage and determination. The architects of the American Revolution, the Founding Fathers, laid the groundwork for a new nation based on the principles of liberty, equality, and self-governance. Their triumphs and sacrifices continue to resonate today, reminding us of the enduring legacy of the American Revolution.

2.2 The Battle for Independence

The Battle for Independence was a pivotal moment in American history, marking the beginning of the Revolutionary War and the fight for freedom from British rule. This section explores the challenges and triumphs faced by the Founding Fathers during this critical period.

The Road to Revolution

Before the Battle for Independence, tensions between the American colonies and Great Britain had been simmering for years. The colonists were growing increasingly frustrated with British policies and taxation without representation. The Stamp Act of 1765 and the Townshend Acts of 1767 were met with widespread resistance, leading to boycotts and protests.

The turning point came in 1774 with the passage of the Intolerable Acts, a series of punitive measures imposed by the British government in response to the Boston Tea Party. These acts further fueled the flames of rebellion and united the colonies in their opposition to British rule.

The Declaration of Independence

On July 4, 1776, the Continental Congress adopted the Declaration of Independence, a document drafted primarily by Thomas Jefferson. This historic declaration proclaimed the colonies' separation from Great Britain and asserted their right to self-governance. It was a bold and revolutionary statement that laid the foundation for the Battle for Independence.

The signing of the Declaration of Independence was a momentous occasion, but it also marked the beginning of a long and arduous struggle. The Founding Fathers knew that their words would be put to the test on the battlefield.

The Battle of Lexington and Concord

The first shots of the Revolutionary War were fired on April 19, 1775, in Lexington and Concord, Massachusetts. British troops were sent to seize colonial weapons and arrest rebel leaders, but they were met with resistance from local militias. The skirmishes that ensued became known as the Battle of Lexington and Concord.

Although the colonial militias were initially outnumbered and outgunned, they displayed remarkable determination and courage. The British forces were forced to retreat, and this early victory boosted the morale of the American revolutionaries.

The Siege of Boston

Following the Battle of Lexington and Concord, the British army found themselves besieged in Boston by colonial forces. Under the leadership of General George Washington, the Continental Army laid siege to the city, cutting off British supply lines and gradually tightening their grip.

The Siege of Boston lasted for nearly a year, from April 1775 to March 1776. During this time, the Continental Army gained valuable experience and honed their military tactics. The successful outcome of the siege demonstrated the resilience and determination of the American forces.

The Battle of Saratoga

One of the most significant turning points in the Revolutionary War was the Battle of Saratoga in 1777. British General John Burgoyne led a campaign to divide the colonies by capturing Albany, New York. However, he was met with fierce resistance from American forces led by General Horatio Gates and Benedict Arnold.

The Battle of Saratoga resulted in a decisive American victory, with Burgoyne's army surrendering on October 17, 1777. This victory not only boosted American morale but also convinced France to formally ally with the United States, providing crucial military and financial support.

The Winter at Valley Forge

The winter of 1777-1778 was a challenging period for the Continental Army. Stationed at Valley Forge, Pennsylvania, the troops faced harsh conditions, including food shortages, inadequate shelter, and disease. Many soldiers succumbed to illness and malnutrition.

Despite these hardships, the soldiers persevered under the leadership of General Washington. The training and discipline instilled during this difficult winter would prove instrumental in future battles. The resilience displayed at Valley Forge demonstrated the unwavering commitment of the American forces to the cause of independence.

The Battle of Yorktown

The Battle of Yorktown in 1781 marked the final major military engagement of the Revolutionary War. American and French forces, led by General Washington and General Rochambeau, laid siege to the British army under General Cornwallis in Yorktown, Virginia.

After weeks of intense fighting, Cornwallis was forced to surrender on October 19, 1781. This victory effectively ended the war and secured American independence. The Battle of Yorktown showcased the military prowess and strategic brilliance of the American and French forces, as well as the determination of the Founding Fathers to achieve victory.

The Legacy of the Revolutionary War

The Battle for Independence was a defining moment in American history, shaping the nation's identity and setting the stage for the creation of a new government. The triumphs and sacrifices of the Founding Fathers during this period laid the groundwork for the principles and values that would guide the United States for centuries to come.

The Revolutionary War not only secured American independence but also inspired other nations around the world to fight for their own freedom. The principles of liberty, equality, and self-governance espoused by the Founding Fathers continue to resonate and inspire people across the globe.

However, the war also had its consequences. The conflict left the young nation in a state of economic instability and political uncertainty. The Founding Fathers would face new challenges as they worked to establish a stable government and navigate the complexities of nation-building.

In the next section, we will explore the price of freedom and the challenges faced by the Founding Fathers as they sought to build a new nation from the ashes of war.

2.3 The Price of Freedom

The Revolutionary War was a pivotal moment in American history, marking the birth of a new nation and the triumph of the American colonies over British rule. However, this victory did not come without a price. The price of freedom was paid in blood, sacrifice, and the immense challenges faced by the Founding Fathers and the American people.

The Sacrifices of War

The Revolutionary War was a long and arduous conflict that lasted for eight years, from 1775 to 1783. The American colonies, led by the Founding Fathers, faced a formidable opponent in the British Empire, which possessed a powerful military and vast resources. The war brought about immense hardships for the American people, as they fought against a superior force for their independence.

The price of freedom was paid by the soldiers who fought on the front lines. These brave men, many of whom were farmers, merchants, and tradesmen, left their families and livelihoods behind to join the Continental Army. They endured harsh conditions, disease, and the constant threat of death on the battlefield. Thousands of soldiers made the ultimate sacrifice, laying down their lives for the cause of liberty.

Financial Burdens and Economic Challenges

The cost of waging war was not only measured in lives lost but also in the economic toll it took on the American colonies. Financing the war effort was a constant struggle for the Founding Fathers. They had to find ways to fund the army, purchase weapons and supplies, and maintain the infrastructure necessary for the war.

To finance the war, the Continental Congress issued paper money known as "Continental currency." However, due to inflation and lack of confidence in the currency, it quickly lost its value, leading to economic instability and hardship for the American people. The war also disrupted trade and commerce, further straining the economy.

The Founding Fathers faced the challenge of managing the financial burdens of war while also ensuring the stability and prosperity of the new nation. This led to debates and discussions on economic policies and the role of government in regulating the economy, which would shape the future of the United States.

Social Disruptions and Personal Sacrifices

The Revolutionary War brought about significant social disruptions and personal sacrifices for the American people. Many families were torn apart as husbands, fathers, and sons went off to fight in the war. Women took on new roles and responsibilities, managing households, farms, and businesses in the absence of their male counterparts.

The war also had a profound impact on enslaved African Americans. While some Founding Fathers, such as Thomas Jefferson, owned slaves, others, like Benjamin Franklin and John Adams, were vocal opponents of slavery. The war presented enslaved individuals with the opportunity to escape bondage and fight for their own freedom. However, the issue of slavery would continue to divide the nation long after the war ended.

The Legacy of the Revolutionary War

The Revolutionary War was a turning point in history, marking the birth of a new nation and the triumph of the American colonies over British rule. The Founding Fathers, through their leadership and determination, laid the foundation for a democratic government that would become a beacon of freedom and inspiration for people around the world.

However, the price of freedom was not limited to the sacrifices made during the war. The challenges faced by the Founding Fathers in establishing a new government, managing the economy, and addressing social issues would shape the course of American history. The legacy of the Revolutionary War can be seen in the Constitution, the Bill of Rights, and the principles of liberty and equality that continue to guide the nation.

27

The price of freedom was high, but the triumphs and consequences of the Revolutionary War paved the way for the United States to become the greatest nation in history. The sacrifices made by the Founding Fathers and the American people serve as a reminder of the enduring values and principles that define the nation to this day.

2.4 The Legacy of the Revolutionary War

The Revolutionary War was a pivotal moment in American history, marking the birth of a new nation and the triumph of the American colonies over British rule. The legacy of this war extends far beyond the battlefield, shaping the future of the United States and leaving a lasting impact on its society, politics, and identity.

The Birth of a Nation

The Revolutionary War not only secured American independence but also laid the foundation for the formation of a new nation. The Founding Fathers, driven by their vision of a democratic society, fought against British oppression and established the principles that would guide the United States for centuries to come. The war served as a catalyst for the creation of a new government and the drafting of the Constitution, which would shape the nation's political structure and ensure the protection of individual rights.

The Ideals of the Revolution

The Revolutionary War was fought not only for independence but also for the ideals of liberty, equality, and self-governance. The Founding Fathers believed in the inherent rights of individuals and sought to create a society where all citizens could participate in the decision-making process. The legacy of the war lies in the enduring principles enshrined in the Declaration of Independence, which proclaimed that "all men are created equal" and endowed with certain unalienable rights.

The Price of Freedom

The Revolutionary War came at a great cost, both in terms of human lives and economic resources. The Founding Fathers and their fellow patriots faced immense challenges and sacrifices during the war. Many lost their lives, their homes, and their livelihoods in the pursuit of freedom. The legacy of the war is a reminder of the courage and resilience of those who fought for independence, as well as the sacrifices made by ordinary citizens who supported the cause.

Shaping the American Identity

The Revolutionary War played a crucial role in shaping the American identity. It instilled a sense of patriotism and national pride among the American people, who saw themselves as a united front against British tyranny. The war also fostered a spirit of innovation and self-reliance, as the colonists had to develop their own military strategies and resources to overcome the powerful British forces. This spirit of independence and resourcefulness would become defining characteristics of the American people.

The Legacy of the Founding Fathers

The Founding Fathers, as the architects of the American Revolution, left a profound legacy that continues to shape the nation to this day. Their commitment to democratic principles and individual rights laid the groundwork for the development of American democracy. The Constitution, drafted by these visionary leaders, established a system of government that has endured for over two centuries, providing a framework for the nation's governance and ensuring the protection of citizens' rights.

Lessons Learned

The legacy of the Revolutionary War offers valuable lessons for future generations. It teaches us the importance of standing up for our beliefs and fighting for what is right, even in the face of overwhelming odds. The Founding Fathers' unwavering commitment to their ideals serves as a reminder that change and progress often require sacrifice and perseverance. The war also highlights the significance of unity and collaboration, as the American colonies were able to achieve victory through collective action and cooperation.

Conclusion

The legacy of the Revolutionary War is a testament to the resilience, determination, and vision of the Founding Fathers. Their triumphs and sacrifices paved the way for the creation of a new nation, founded on the principles of liberty, equality, and self-governance. The war not only secured American independence but also shaped the nation's identity and political structure. The lessons learned from this pivotal moment in history continue to resonate today, reminding us of the enduring importance of freedom, democracy, and the pursuit of a more perfect union.

The Creation of a New Government

3.1 The Constitutional Convention

The Constitutional Convention, held in Philadelphia from May 25 to September 17, 1787, was a pivotal event in American history. It brought together delegates from the thirteen states to address the weaknesses of the Articles of Confederation and create a new framework for governing the nation. The convention was a remarkable gathering of some of the brightest minds and influential figures of the time, known as the Founding Fathers.

The Need for a New Constitution

The Articles of Confederation, which had served as the first constitution of the United States, proved to be inadequate in effectively governing the young nation. The central government lacked the power to tax, regulate commerce, or enforce laws, leading to economic instability and political disarray. Recognizing the need for a stronger central government, the delegates convened to draft a new constitution that would establish a more balanced and effective system of governance.

The Delegates

The Constitutional Convention brought together fifty-five delegates from twelve of the thirteen states (Rhode Island did not send any representatives). These delegates were a diverse group, including lawyers, merchants, plantation owners, and military leaders. Among them were some of the most prominent figures in American history, such as George Washington, Benjamin Franklin, James Madison, Alexander Hamilton, and Thomas Jefferson (although Jefferson did not attend the convention as he was serving as the United States Minister to France at the time).

The Virginia and New Jersey Plans

The convention began with a debate over the structure of the new government. Two competing plans emerged: the Virginia Plan and the New Jersey Plan.

The Virginia Plan, proposed by James Madison, called for a strong central government with a bicameral legislature and representation based on population. This plan favored the larger states. In contrast, the New Jersey Plan, put forth by William Paterson, advocated for a unicameral legislature with equal representation for all states, regardless of size. This plan aimed to protect the interests of the smaller states.

The Great Compromise

The debate between the Virginia and New Jersey Plans threatened to derail the convention. However, a compromise was reached, known as the Great Compromise or the Connecticut Compromise. It proposed a bicameral legislature, with the House of Representatives based on population and the Senate granting equal representation to each state. This compromise satisfied both the larger and smaller states and laid the foundation for the structure of the United States Congress that we have today.

Other Key Debates and Compromises

The delegates at the Constitutional Convention grappled with numerous other contentious issues. One of the most significant was the debate over slavery. Southern states, reliant on the institution of slavery, sought to protect their interests, while delegates from the North pushed for its abolition. The Three-Fifths Compromise was eventually reached, which counted each enslaved person as three-fifths of a person for the purposes of representation and taxation.

Another crucial debate centered around the balance of power between the federal government and the states. The delegates sought to strike a delicate balance, ensuring a strong central government while preserving the rights and autonomy of the states. The result was a system of federalism, where power is divided between the national government and the states.

The Drafting of the Constitution

Over the course of the convention, the delegates worked tirelessly to draft the Constitution of the United States. James Madison, often referred to as the "Father of the Constitution," played a significant role in shaping its content. The final document established a framework for a federal government with three branches: the legislative, executive, and judicial. It outlined the powers and responsibilities of each branch and provided a system of checks and balances to prevent the abuse of power.

Ratification and the Bill of Rights

After the Constitution was drafted, it faced the challenge of ratification. The document required approval from at least nine of the thirteen states to become law. This process sparked intense debates and public discussions across the nation. Supporters of the Constitution, known as Federalists, argued for its adoption, while opponents, known as Anti-Federalists, raised concerns about the potential for a centralized government to infringe upon individual liberties.

To address these concerns, the promise of a Bill of Rights was made. The Bill of Rights, consisting of the first ten amendments to the Constitution, guaranteed individual freedoms and limited the power of the federal government. It played a crucial role in securing the ratification of the Constitution and remains a cornerstone of American democracy.

The Legacy of the Constitutional Convention

The Constitutional Convention was a remarkable achievement that laid the foundation for the United States of America as we know it today. The delegates' ability to navigate complex issues and reach compromises demonstrated their commitment to creating a government that would endure. The Constitution they drafted has stood the test of time, providing a framework for democratic governance and serving as a model for nations around the world.

The Constitutional Convention also highlighted the brilliance and foresight of the Founding Fathers. Their collective wisdom and dedication to the principles of liberty, equality, and justice shaped the course of American history. While they were not without flaws and contradictions, their contributions to the creation of a new government cannot be overstated. The Constitution they crafted continues to guide and inspire generations of Americans, reminding us of the triumphs and consequences of their visionary work.

3.2 Debates and Compromises

The creation of a new government for the United States of America was not a straightforward process. It involved intense debates and numerous compromises among the Founding Fathers. These debates and compromises were essential in shaping the structure and principles of the new nation.

One of the most significant debates during the Constitutional Convention was the issue of representation. The larger states, such as Virginia and Pennsylvania, argued for representation based on population, while the smaller states, like Delaware and New Jersey, feared being overshadowed and advocated for equal representation for all states. This debate led to the creation of the Great Compromise, also known as the Connecticut Compromise, which established a bicameral legislature. The House of Representatives would be based on population, satisfying the larger states, while the Senate would have equal representation for each state, appeasing the smaller states.

Another contentious issue was the question of slavery. The Founding Fathers were aware of the moral dilemma posed by slavery, but they also recognized the economic importance of the institution to the Southern states. This led to heated debates and compromises that sought to balance the interests of both sides. The Three-Fifths Compromise was reached, which determined that enslaved individuals would be counted as three-fifths of a person for the purposes of representation and taxation. This compromise appeased the Southern states, as it gave them greater representation in Congress, while also acknowledging the humanity of enslaved individuals to some extent.

The issue of slavery also intersected with the debate over the regulation of commerce. Northern states, which had fewer economic ties to slavery, sought to empower the federal government to regulate and potentially abolish the slave trade. However, the Southern states, heavily reliant on slavery, vehemently opposed any interference in their economic practices. To reach a compromise, the Founding Fathers agreed to postpone any legislation regarding the international slave trade for twenty years, allowing the Southern states to continue their practices while giving the Northern states hope for future change.

Another significant debate centered around the balance of power between the federal government and the states. Some Founding Fathers, like Alexander Hamilton, believed in a strong central government, while others, such as Thomas Jefferson, championed states' rights. This debate led to the creation of the system of federalism, where power is divided between the federal government and the states. The Constitution granted certain powers to the federal government while reserving others for the states, striking a delicate balance that has endured to this day.

The debates and compromises during the Constitutional Convention were not limited to these issues alone. There were discussions on the length of the presidential term, the method of electing the president, and the inclusion of a Bill of Rights, among other topics. Each decision required careful consideration and negotiation to ensure the unity and stability of the new nation.

The Founding Fathers understood the importance of compromise in the creation of a functional government. They recognized that no single faction could have their way entirely without alienating others and risking the collapse of the entire endeavor. Through their willingness to engage in debates and make compromises, they laid the foundation for a government that could adapt and evolve over time.

The compromises made during the Constitutional Convention were not without consequences. The Three-Fifths Compromise, while a temporary solution, perpetuated the institution of slavery and deepened the divide between the North and the South. The decision to postpone the regulation of the international slave trade allowed the practice to continue for two more decades, prolonging the suffering of enslaved individuals.

However, the compromises also allowed for the creation of a government that could function and address the needs of a diverse nation. The Great Compromise ensured that both large and small states had a voice in the legislative process. The system of federalism struck a balance between a strong central government and the autonomy of the states.

The debates and compromises of the Founding Fathers were not perfect, and they did not solve all the challenges facing the new nation. However, they laid the groundwork for a government that could adapt and grow, allowing future generations to address the triumphs and consequences of their decisions. The debates and compromises of the Founding Fathers continue to shape the United States of America, reminding us of the importance of dialogue, negotiation, and compromise in the pursuit of a more perfect union.

3.3 Ratification and the Bill of Rights

After the Constitutional Convention concluded in September 1787, the proposed Constitution faced a significant hurdle: ratification by the states. The Founding Fathers understood that without the support of the states, the Constitution would be nothing more than a well-crafted document. The process of ratification was a crucial step in solidifying the new government and ensuring its legitimacy.

The Debate over Ratification

The ratification process sparked intense debates across the states. Two factions emerged: the Federalists, who supported the Constitution, and the Anti-Federalists, who opposed it. The Federalists, led by Alexander Hamilton, James Madison, and John Jay, argued that the Constitution provided a strong central government necessary for the stability and prosperity of the nation. They believed that the Constitution struck a delicate balance between state and federal powers, ensuring both the protection of individual rights and the ability to govern effectively.

On the other hand, the Anti-Federalists, including prominent figures like Patrick Henry and George Mason, feared that the Constitution granted too much power to the federal government at the expense of the states. They worried that the absence of a Bill of Rights would leave individual liberties vulnerable to infringement. The Anti-Federalists argued that the Constitution needed explicit protections for individual rights to prevent the government from becoming tyrannical.

The Federalist Papers

To sway public opinion in favor of ratification, the Federalists authored a series of essays known as the Federalist Papers. Alexander Hamilton, James Madison, and John Jay wrote these essays under the pseudonym "Publius."

The Federalist Papers provided a comprehensive defense of the Constitution, addressing concerns raised by the Anti-Federalists.

In these essays, the Federalists argued that the separation of powers, checks and balances, and the federal structure of government would prevent any one branch or entity from becoming too powerful. They also emphasized the importance of a strong central government to maintain order and protect the nation's interests. The Federalist Papers played a crucial role in shaping public opinion and garnering support for the Constitution.

The Compromise: The Bill of Rights

Despite the Federalists' efforts, many states were still hesitant to ratify the Constitution without explicit protections for individual rights. To address these concerns, James Madison proposed a series of amendments to the Constitution, which would become known as the Bill of Rights. Madison drew inspiration from state constitutions and the English Bill of Rights of 1689.

The Bill of Rights, consisting of ten amendments, was designed to safeguard individual liberties and limit the power of the federal government. These amendments protected fundamental rights such as freedom of speech, religion, and the press, the right to bear arms, and protection against unreasonable searches and seizures. They also established due process rights, including the right to a fair trial and protection against self-incrimination.

The inclusion of the Bill of Rights was a significant compromise that helped secure the ratification of the Constitution. It reassured the Anti-Federalists that the new government would respect and protect individual rights. The Bill of Rights became an integral part of the Constitution, ensuring that the government would be accountable to the people and preventing the concentration of power.

Ratification and the Birth of a New Government

Delaware became the first state to ratify the Constitution on December 7, 1787, followed by Pennsylvania, New Jersey, Georgia, and Connecticut. However, the road to ratification was not without obstacles. In states like Massachusetts, New York, and Virginia, the ratification process faced fierce opposition. It was only through intense debates, compromises, and the promise of a Bill of Rights that these states eventually ratified the Constitution.

On June 21, 1788, New Hampshire became the ninth state to ratify the Constitution, reaching the required threshold for the Constitution to take effect. The new government began operating under the Constitution on March 4, 1789, with the inauguration of George Washington as the first President of the United States.

The ratification of the Constitution marked a significant triumph for the Founding Fathers. They had successfully created a framework for a new government that balanced power between the states and the federal government while protecting individual rights. The inclusion of the Bill of Rights ensured that the government would be accountable to the people and prevented the potential abuse of power.

The ratification process and the subsequent adoption of the Bill of Rights demonstrated the Founding Fathers' commitment to creating a government that respected the principles of liberty and justice. Their foresight and willingness to compromise laid the foundation for the enduring success of the United States of America.

3.4 The Birth of the American Presidency

The birth of the American presidency was a pivotal moment in the history of the United States. It marked the establishment of a new form of government and the beginning of a unique experiment in democracy. The Founding Fathers, in their wisdom, recognized the need for a strong executive branch to lead the nation and ensure its stability and prosperity. In this section, we will explore the origins of the American presidency, the debates surrounding its creation, and the lasting impact it has had on the nation.

The Need for Executive Leadership

During the Constitutional Convention of 1787, the Founding Fathers grappled with the question of how to structure the new government. They recognized the importance of having a single individual at the helm who could provide decisive leadership and represent the nation both domestically and internationally. The presidency was seen as a crucial component of the checks and balances system that would prevent the concentration of power and protect the rights of the people.

The Powers and Responsibilities of the President

The delegates at the Constitutional Convention debated extensively on the powers and responsibilities of the president. They sought to strike a delicate balance between granting the executive branch enough authority to effectively govern and ensuring that it remained accountable to the people. The president was given the power to veto legislation, command the military, and negotiate treaties, among other responsibilities. However, the Constitution also established a system of checks and balances, with Congress and the judiciary serving as counterweights to the president's power.

The Election of the President

One of the most contentious issues surrounding the creation of the presidency was the method of election. The Founding Fathers debated whether the president should be elected by Congress or directly by the people. Ultimately, they settled on the Electoral College system, which combined elements of both approaches. Under this system, each state would appoint a number of electors equal to its representation in Congress, who would then vote for the president. This compromise was intended to ensure that the president would be chosen by a body of knowledgeable individuals while still maintaining a connection to the will of the people.

The First Presidents

The first president of the United States, George Washington, set important precedents for the office. He established the tradition of a two-term presidency, which would later become an unwritten rule until it was codified into law with the 22nd Amendment in 1951. Washington also played a crucial role in shaping the presidency by exercising restraint and avoiding the abuse of power. His leadership and statesmanship laid the foundation for future presidents to follow.

The Evolution of the Presidency

Over the years, the presidency has evolved and expanded in response to the changing needs and challenges of the nation. The powers and responsibilities of the president have grown, particularly in times of crisis or war. For example, Abraham Lincoln's presidency during the Civil War saw an expansion of executive authority as he took measures to preserve the Union. Similarly, Franklin D. Roosevelt's presidency during the Great Depression and World War II saw the implementation of sweeping economic and social reforms.

The Impact of the American Presidency

The American presidency has had a profound impact on the nation and the world. It has served as a symbol of American democracy and leadership, representing the ideals and aspirations of the nation. The president has the power to shape public opinion, set the policy agenda, and make critical decisions that can have far-reaching consequences. The presidency has also become a focal point of political and cultural debates, with each new administration bringing its own vision and priorities to the office.

Challenges and Criticisms

While the American presidency has been a source of strength and stability, it has also faced its share of challenges and criticisms. Some have argued that the presidency has become too powerful, with presidents exceeding their constitutional authority and bypassing Congress. Others have criticized the Electoral College system, arguing that it can lead to the election of a president who did not win the popular vote. Additionally, the presidency has been criticized for its lack of diversity, with the majority of presidents being white men.

Conclusion

The birth of the American presidency was a momentous event in the history of the United States. It represented the culmination of the Founding Fathers' vision for a strong and accountable executive branch. Over the years, the presidency has evolved and adapted to the changing needs of the nation, shaping the course of American history. While it has faced challenges and criticisms, the presidency remains a symbol of American democracy and leadership, embodying the ideals and aspirations of the nation.

The Founding Fathers and Slavery

4.1 The Paradox of Liberty

The Founding Fathers of the United States were men of great intellect and vision. They were driven by a desire to create a nation that would be a beacon of liberty and equality for all. However, there was a glaring paradox at the heart of their endeavor - the institution of slavery. While these men championed the ideals of freedom and justice, many of them were also slaveholders. This contradiction raises important questions about the true nature of their commitment to liberty.

The paradox of liberty becomes evident when we examine the lives and actions of the Founding Fathers. On one hand, they were instrumental in drafting and signing documents such as the Declaration of Independence, which declared that "all men are created equal" and endowed with certain unalienable rights. On the other hand, many of these same men owned slaves and perpetuated a system that denied basic human rights to a significant portion of the population.

Thomas Jefferson, one of the primary architects of the Declaration of Independence, is a prime example of this paradox. Jefferson famously wrote, "We hold these truths to be self-evident, that all men are created equal." Yet, he owned over 600 slaves throughout his lifetime. This contradiction has led to much debate and scrutiny of Jefferson's legacy. How can a man who espoused such lofty ideals also participate in the institution of slavery?

The answer lies in the complex social and economic realities of the time. Slavery was deeply ingrained in the fabric of American society, particularly in the southern states where agriculture, particularly the cultivation of cash crops like tobacco and cotton, relied heavily on slave labor. Many of the Founding Fathers, including Jefferson, were born into a world where slavery was an accepted and widespread practice. They inherited slaves through family estates and saw them as essential to their economic prosperity.

However, it is important to note that not all of the Founding Fathers were slaveholders. Some, like John Adams and Alexander Hamilton, were staunch opponents of slavery. They recognized the inherent contradiction between the principles of liberty and the institution of slavery. Adams, in particular, was an early advocate for the abolition of slavery and believed that it was incompatible with the ideals of the American Revolution.

Despite the presence of abolitionist voices among the Founding Fathers, the institution of slavery persisted and even expanded in the years following the American Revolution. The Constitution, which was drafted and signed by many of these men, contained compromises that protected the interests of slaveholding states. The infamous Three-Fifths Compromise, for example, counted enslaved individuals as three-fifths of a person for the purposes of determining representation in Congress.

The consequences of this paradox of liberty were far-reaching. Slavery continued to divide the nation and sow the seeds of future conflict. The issue of slavery would eventually lead to the Civil War, the bloodiest conflict in American history. The legacy of slavery and its impact on African Americans and the nation as a whole cannot be overstated.

It is important to recognize and grapple with this paradox when studying the Founding Fathers. While they were undoubtedly brilliant and visionary men who laid the foundation for the United States, they were also products of their time and subject to the prevailing attitudes and practices of the era. Their commitment to liberty and equality was often limited by the constraints of their own circumstances.

In conclusion, the paradox of liberty is a central aspect of the Founding Fathers' legacy. While they championed the ideals of freedom and equality, many of them were also slaveholders. This contradiction raises important questions about the true nature of their commitment to liberty. Understanding this paradox is crucial for a comprehensive understanding of the complexities and contradictions of America's founding era.

4.2 Slaveholding Founders

The issue of slavery is one of the most complex and controversial aspects of American history. While the Founding Fathers are often revered for their role in establishing the principles of liberty and equality, it is important to acknowledge that many of them were slaveholders themselves. This section will explore the uncomfortable truth that some of the men who laid the foundation for American democracy also participated in the institution of slavery.

The Paradox of Liberty

The Founding Fathers faced a profound contradiction when it came to the issue of slavery. On one hand, they championed the ideals of freedom and equality, as expressed in the Declaration of Independence. On the other hand, many of them owned slaves and benefited from the labor and wealth generated by the institution.

Thomas Jefferson, the principal author of the Declaration of Independence, is perhaps the most well-known example of a slaveholding founder. Despite his eloquent words about the inalienable rights of all men, Jefferson owned over 600 slaves throughout his lifetime. This contradiction has led to much debate and criticism of Jefferson's legacy.

Slaveholding Founders

Jefferson was not alone in his ownership of slaves among the Founding Fathers. George Washington, the first President of the United States, also owned slaves. At the time of his death, Washington had over 300 slaves on his Mount Vernon plantation. Other prominent slaveholding founders include James Madison, James Monroe, and Benjamin Franklin.

The reasons for their participation in slavery varied. Some inherited slaves from their families, while others purchased them as a means of economic prosperity. Slavery was deeply ingrained in the fabric of society at the time, and it was not uncommon for individuals to view it as a necessary evil or a means of maintaining their social and economic status.

The Dilemma of Abolition

While some of the Founding Fathers owned slaves, it is important to note that not all of them supported the institution. There were those who recognized the moral and ethical contradictions of slavery and actively sought its abolition.

One such founder was John Adams, who never owned slaves and was an outspoken critic of the institution. Adams believed that slavery was incompatible with the principles of the American Revolution and advocated for its gradual abolition. However, his efforts were met with resistance from other founders who feared the economic and social consequences of emancipation.

The Legacy of Slavery

The legacy of slavery continues to shape American society to this day. The institution had a profound impact on the economic, social, and political development of the United States. Slavery fueled the growth of the Southern economy, particularly in agriculture, and contributed to the widening divide between the North and the South.

The Founding Fathers' involvement in slavery raises important questions about the nature of their vision for America. How could men who espoused the principles of liberty and equality also participate in the subjugation of an entire race? This paradox has led to ongoing debates about the true intentions and motivations of the Founding Fathers.

It is crucial to recognize that the Founding Fathers were not infallible. They were products of their time, shaped by the prevailing attitudes and beliefs of the era. While their contributions to the establishment of the United States cannot be denied, it is essential to acknowledge their flaws and contradictions.

In conclusion, the Founding Fathers were not a monolithic group when it came to the issue of slavery. Some owned slaves and perpetuated the institution, while others recognized its inherent injustice and sought its abolition. The legacy of slavery continues to be a painful and complex part of American history, reminding us of the ongoing struggle for equality and justice.

4.3 Abolitionist Founders

While it is widely known that many of the Founding Fathers were slaveholders, it is important to recognize that there were also Founding Fathers who actively opposed slavery and advocated for its abolition. These abolitionist Founders played a significant role in shaping the discourse around slavery and laying the groundwork for its eventual eradication in the United States. This section will explore the lives and contributions of some of these remarkable individuals.

John Adams

John Adams, the second President of the United States, was an early advocate for the abolition of slavery. He believed that slavery was morally wrong and incompatible with the principles of liberty and equality upon which the nation was founded. Adams was a vocal critic of the institution and spoke out against it throughout his political career. In 1777, he drafted a provision for the Massachusetts Constitution that would have abolished slavery in the state, but it was ultimately rejected. Despite this setback, Adams continued to express his opposition to slavery and worked towards its eventual abolition.

Benjamin Franklin

Benjamin Franklin, one of the most influential Founding Fathers, also became an outspoken opponent of slavery later in his life. Franklin initially owned slaves but eventually came to view slavery as a grave injustice. In 1787, he became the president of the Pennsylvania Society for Promoting the Abolition of Slavery, an organization dedicated to ending slavery in the state. Franklin used his platform to advocate for the rights of enslaved individuals and to raise awareness about the horrors of the slave trade. His efforts helped to galvanize the abolitionist movement and bring the issue of slavery to the forefront of public consciousness.

Alexander Hamilton

Alexander Hamilton, a key figure in the formation of the United States'
financial system, was also an abolitionist. While Hamilton did not own slaves
himself, he recognized the inherent contradiction between the principles of the
American Revolution and the institution of slavery. He believed that slavery
was not only morally wrong but also economically detrimental to the nation.
Hamilton actively supported the abolitionist cause and worked alongside other
like-minded individuals to promote the gradual emancipation of slaves.
Although his efforts were not successful during his lifetime, Hamilton's
advocacy for abolition laid the groundwork for future generations of
abolitionists.

John Jay

John Jay, the first Chief Justice of the United States, was another prominent
abolitionist Founder. Jay was a staunch opponent of slavery and used his
position to advance the cause of abolition. In 1777, he drafted a law that would
have abolished slavery in New York, but it was not passed by the state
legislature. Jay also served as the president of the New York Manumission
Society, an organization dedicated to the gradual emancipation of slaves.
Through his writings and activism, Jay sought to challenge the prevailing
attitudes towards slavery and promote the idea that all individuals, regardless
of race, were entitled to freedom and equality.

Thomas Paine

Thomas Paine, a political activist and author of influential works such as
"Common Sense," was an early advocate for the abolition of slavery. Paine
believed that slavery was a violation of natural rights and argued that it was
incompatible with the principles of the American Revolution. In his essay,
"African Slavery in America," Paine condemned the institution of slavery and
called for its immediate abolition. His writings helped to shape public opinion
and raise awareness about the injustices of slavery.

These abolitionist Founding Fathers, among others, played a crucial role in challenging the institution of slavery and advocating for its abolition. Their efforts helped to shift public opinion and lay the groundwork for the eventual eradication of slavery in the United States. While their contributions may have been overshadowed by the actions of their slaveholding counterparts, it is important to recognize and celebrate their commitment to the principles of liberty and equality that underpin the American experiment. The legacy of these abolitionist Founders serves as a reminder that progress is possible, even in the face of seemingly insurmountable challenges.

4.4 The Legacy of Slavery

The legacy of slavery is a dark stain on the history of the United States and a topic that cannot be ignored when discussing the founding fathers. While these men were instrumental in the creation of a new nation and the establishment of its democratic principles, they were also complicit in the institution of slavery. This section will explore the complex and contradictory relationship between the founding fathers and slavery, as well as the lasting impact it had on American society.

Slavery in the Early Republic

At the time of the American Revolution, slavery was deeply entrenched in the fabric of society, particularly in the southern states. Many of the founding fathers themselves were slaveholders, including prominent figures such as George Washington, Thomas Jefferson, and James Madison. These men, who championed the ideals of liberty and equality, were paradoxically involved in the ownership of human beings.

The institution of slavery was not only a moral contradiction but also a political challenge for the founding fathers. The issue of slavery threatened to divide the newly formed nation, as the northern states increasingly moved towards abolition while the southern states relied on slave labor for their agrarian economies. The founding fathers were acutely aware of this tension and struggled to find a solution that would preserve the unity of the country.

The Compromises of the Constitution

During the Constitutional Convention of 1787, the issue of slavery loomed large. The southern states, fearing that their economic interests would be undermined, fought to protect the institution. The result was a series of compromises that allowed slavery to continue while attempting to balance the competing interests of the northern and southern states.

The most notable compromise was the Three-Fifths Compromise, which counted enslaved individuals as three-fifths of a person for the purposes of determining representation in Congress. This compromise not only perpetuated the dehumanization of enslaved people but also gave disproportionate political power to the southern states, as they could count their enslaved population towards their representation.

Abolitionist Founders

While many of the founding fathers were slaveholders, there were also those who opposed the institution of slavery. Benjamin Franklin, for example, became an outspoken critic of slavery later in his life and became actively involved in abolitionist efforts. John Adams, though initially ambivalent about slavery, also expressed his moral opposition to the institution.

However, it is important to note that even those who opposed slavery did not necessarily advocate for immediate emancipation. Many of them believed that the gradual abolition of slavery was a more practical approach, fearing that the sudden emancipation of enslaved people would lead to social and economic upheaval.

The Legacy of Slavery

The legacy of slavery is far-reaching and continues to shape American society to this day. The institution of slavery not only perpetuated the dehumanization and oppression of millions of African Americans but also laid the foundation for systemic racism and inequality that persists in various forms.

The economic prosperity of the southern states was built on the backs of enslaved labor, and the wealth accumulated during this time contributed to the development of the United States as a global power. The cotton industry, in particular, fueled the growth of the American economy and played a significant role in the Industrial Revolution.

The legacy of slavery also had profound social and cultural implications. The racial hierarchy established during slavery continues to influence attitudes and perceptions towards African Americans, leading to ongoing racial disparities in areas such as education, employment, and criminal justice.

The Road to Abolition

The founding fathers' failure to address the issue of slavery directly in the Constitution set the stage for a long and contentious struggle for abolition. Over the following decades, the United States would be torn apart by the issue of slavery, culminating in the Civil War. The Emancipation Proclamation in 1863 and the subsequent ratification of the Thirteenth Amendment in 1865 finally abolished slavery in the United States.

However, the end of slavery did not mark the end of racial discrimination and inequality. The legacy of slavery continued to shape the experiences of African Americans during the Reconstruction era and beyond. Jim Crow laws, segregation, and systemic racism persisted, denying African Americans their full rights and perpetuating a cycle of inequality.

Conclusion

The founding fathers, despite their visionary ideals, were unable to fully confront the moral contradiction of slavery. Their failure to address the issue directly in the Constitution and their compromises to preserve the unity of the nation allowed the institution to persist for generations. The legacy of slavery continues to haunt the United States, reminding us of the deep-rooted inequalities that still need to be addressed. It serves as a reminder that even the most revered figures in history are not immune to the flaws and contradictions of their time.

Foreign Relations and Diplomacy

5.1 The Challenges of a New Nation

The birth of a new nation is never an easy process. It requires immense dedication, sacrifice, and the ability to overcome numerous challenges. The Founding Fathers of the United States were well aware of the difficulties they would face in establishing a new government and forging relationships with other nations. In this section, we will explore the challenges that the young nation encountered in its early years and how the Founding Fathers navigated through them.

One of the primary challenges faced by the United States was its lack of international recognition. The American Revolution had severed ties with Great Britain, but the new nation had yet to establish itself as a legitimate entity in the eyes of the world. The Founding Fathers understood the importance of gaining recognition from other nations, as it would provide economic and diplomatic opportunities. However, achieving this recognition proved to be a daunting task.

The European powers, particularly Great Britain and France, were skeptical of the United States' ability to survive and thrive as an independent nation. They viewed the American Revolution as a rebellion rather than a legitimate movement for independence. Additionally, the European powers were engaged in their own conflicts and had little interest in supporting a fledgling nation across the Atlantic.

To overcome these challenges, the Founding Fathers embarked on a diplomatic campaign to secure recognition and establish relationships with other nations. Benjamin Franklin, John Adams, and Thomas Jefferson played crucial roles in these efforts. They traveled to Europe, engaging in negotiations and diplomacy to convince foreign powers of the United States' legitimacy.

Despite their efforts, the road to international recognition was long and arduous. The United States faced numerous setbacks and rejections. However, the persistence and determination of the Founding Fathers eventually paid off.

In 1778, the United States signed the Treaty of Alliance with France, which provided crucial military and financial support during the Revolutionary War. This alliance not only helped secure American independence but also signaled to other nations that the United States was a force to be reckoned with.

Another significant challenge faced by the young nation was the establishment of a stable economy. The United States had just emerged from a long and costly war, and its economy was in shambles. The Founding Fathers recognized the need for economic stability and growth to ensure the survival of the nation.

Alexander Hamilton, the first Secretary of the Treasury, played a pivotal role in shaping the economic policies of the United States. He advocated for a strong central government and the implementation of a sound financial system. Hamilton's economic plan included the assumption of state debts, the creation of a national bank, and the promotion of manufacturing and industry. These policies were met with resistance from those who favored a more agrarian economy, such as Thomas Jefferson. However, Hamilton's vision ultimately prevailed, laying the foundation for the economic prosperity of the United States.

In addition to economic challenges, the United States also faced territorial disputes and conflicts with other nations. The Louisiana Purchase in 1803 was a significant milestone in the expansion of the United States. President Thomas Jefferson negotiated the purchase of the vast territory from France, doubling the size of the nation. This acquisition not only provided valuable resources and land but also solidified the United States' position as a continental power.

However, territorial expansion also brought about conflicts with Native American tribes and neighboring nations. The War of 1812, fought between the United States and Great Britain, was a direct result of these territorial disputes. The war had significant consequences for the young nation, including the burning of Washington, D.C., and the emergence of national symbols such as "The Star-Spangled Banner."

Despite the challenges faced by the United States in its early years, the Founding Fathers were able to navigate through them with resilience and determination. Their diplomatic efforts secured international recognition, their economic policies laid the foundation for prosperity, and their territorial expansion solidified the nation's position on the world stage. The challenges faced by the young nation served as a crucible, forging a united and resilient America that would go on to become the greatest nation in history.

5.2 The Founders and European Powers

The Founding Fathers of the United States were not only concerned with establishing a new nation and crafting a constitution, but they also had to navigate the complex world of international relations. In the aftermath of the Revolutionary War, the young United States found itself in a precarious position, surrounded by powerful European powers who were eager to assert their influence. This section explores the interactions between the Founding Fathers and European powers, shedding light on the challenges they faced and the consequences of their decisions.

The Post-Revolutionary War Landscape

Following the victory in the Revolutionary War, the United States emerged as a new nation on the world stage. However, it was not immediately recognized as an independent country by the European powers. The Founding Fathers, aware of the need to secure international recognition and establish diplomatic relations, embarked on a series of diplomatic efforts.

The Founders and Great Britain

One of the most significant challenges the Founding Fathers faced was dealing with their former colonial ruler, Great Britain. Despite the signing of the Treaty of Paris in 1783, which officially recognized American independence, tensions between the two nations persisted. The British maintained a strong presence in North America, particularly in Canada, and were reluctant to fully acknowledge the United States as a sovereign nation.

The Founding Fathers, led by figures such as Benjamin Franklin and John Adams, engaged in diplomatic negotiations with the British government to establish trade relations and resolve outstanding issues. The Jay Treaty of 1794, negotiated by Chief Justice John Jay, aimed to address some of these concerns. It sought to resolve disputes over trade, boundaries, and the presence of British troops in the Northwest Territory. While the treaty was met with criticism from some quarters, it helped to ease tensions between the United States and Great Britain.

The Founders and France

France played a crucial role in supporting the American Revolution, providing military aid and crucial assistance in securing victory. However, the relationship between the United States and France became strained in the aftermath of the war. The French Revolution, which erupted in 1789, further complicated matters.

The Founding Fathers, particularly Thomas Jefferson, had a deep affinity for France and its revolutionary ideals. However, they also recognized the need to maintain a delicate balance between their support for France and their desire to establish stable relations with other European powers. The signing of the Jay Treaty with Great Britain, which was seen as a betrayal by the French, further strained the relationship.

The Founders and Spain

Spain, with its vast territories in North America, posed another challenge for the United States. The Mississippi River and the port of New Orleans were crucial for American trade, and the Founding Fathers sought to secure access to these vital waterways. Negotiations with Spain proved to be complex and protracted.

In 1795, the United States and Spain signed the Treaty of San Lorenzo, also known as Pinckney's Treaty. This treaty granted the United States the right to navigate the Mississippi River and use the port of New Orleans for trade. It also established the boundary between Spanish Florida and the United States. The treaty was a significant diplomatic victory for the Founding Fathers, as it secured vital trade routes and helped to stabilize relations with Spain.

The Founders and Other European Powers

Beyond Great Britain, France, and Spain, the Founding Fathers also had to contend with the interests and ambitions of other European powers. Nations such as Russia, Prussia, and the Netherlands sought to establish diplomatic ties with the United States and expand their influence in North America.

The Founding Fathers, aware of the need to balance these competing interests, engaged in diplomatic efforts to establish relations with these nations. Treaties were signed, diplomatic missions were dispatched, and efforts were made to secure trade agreements. These interactions helped to solidify the United States' position as a sovereign nation and establish its place in the international community.

Consequences and Legacy

The interactions between the Founding Fathers and European powers had far-reaching consequences for the young United States. The diplomatic efforts of figures such as Benjamin Franklin, John Adams, and Thomas Jefferson helped to secure recognition and establish the United States as a legitimate nation.

These diplomatic victories also laid the groundwork for future foreign relations and set a precedent for American diplomacy. The Founding Fathers' commitment to negotiation, compromise, and the pursuit of national interests shaped the way the United States would engage with the world in the years to come.

However, the challenges and complexities of international relations would continue to shape the nation's history. The United States would face further conflicts, such as the War of 1812, which tested its resolve and highlighted the importance of maintaining strong diplomatic ties.

In conclusion, the Founding Fathers' interactions with European powers were crucial in shaping the early years of the United States. Their diplomatic efforts, negotiations, and compromises helped to establish the nation's place in the world and set the stage for future foreign relations. The consequences of their decisions and actions continue to resonate in American diplomacy and international relations to this day.

5.3 The Louisiana Purchase

The Louisiana Purchase stands as one of the most significant events in American history. It was a monumental acquisition that doubled the size of the United States and forever altered the course of the nation. This section explores the circumstances surrounding the Louisiana Purchase, the key players involved, and the consequences it had on the young republic.

The Background

In the early 1800s, the vast territory of Louisiana was under the control of France, led by Napoleon Bonaparte. The region encompassed a vast expanse of land, stretching from the Mississippi River to the Rocky Mountains and from the Gulf of Mexico to the Canadian border. It held strategic importance due to its access to the Mississippi River and the valuable port of New Orleans.

At the time, the United States relied heavily on the Mississippi River for trade, and the port of New Orleans was crucial for the transportation of goods. However, in 1802, Spain, who had previously controlled the Louisiana Territory, secretly transferred it back to France. This transfer raised concerns among American leaders, as they feared that France might restrict their access to the Mississippi River, hindering their economic growth and expansion.

The Negotiations

In an effort to secure American interests, President Thomas Jefferson dispatched James Monroe and Robert Livingston to negotiate with the French government. Their primary objective was to secure the rights to use the port of New Orleans and ensure the free navigation of the Mississippi River.

However, to their surprise, the French offered to sell the entire Louisiana Territory to the United States. Napoleon, facing financial difficulties and the threat of war in Europe, saw an opportunity to divest himself of a distant and potentially troublesome territory. The negotiations were swift, and on April

30, 1803, the Louisiana Purchase Treaty was signed, transferring the vast territory to the United States for the sum of $15 million.

The Consequences

The Louisiana Purchase had far-reaching consequences for the United States. Firstly, it doubled the size of the nation, expanding its borders westward and opening up vast opportunities for settlement and economic growth. The acquisition of this vast territory provided the United States with valuable natural resources, fertile land for agriculture, and access to key trade routes.

Secondly, the Louisiana Purchase removed the threat of a foreign power controlling the Mississippi River and the port of New Orleans. This secured American access to these vital waterways, ensuring the continued growth of trade and commerce.

Furthermore, the Louisiana Purchase had significant geopolitical implications. It removed France as a potential rival power in North America and solidified the United States' position as the dominant force on the continent. The acquisition also set a precedent for future territorial expansion, as it demonstrated the willingness of the United States to pursue its interests through negotiation and acquisition.

However, the Louisiana Purchase also raised questions about the constitutionality of such a large acquisition of territory. President Jefferson, a strict constructionist, had reservations about the legality of the purchase. Nonetheless, he recognized the immense benefits it would bring to the nation and ultimately decided to proceed with the acquisition.

Legacy and Impact

The Louisiana Purchase had a profound and lasting impact on the United States. It paved the way for westward expansion, as settlers began to migrate into the newly acquired territory. The Lewis and Clark Expedition, commissioned by President Jefferson, explored the vast wilderness of the Louisiana Territory, mapping the region and establishing American presence.

The acquisition of Louisiana also had implications for Native American tribes who inhabited the region. As American settlers moved westward, conflicts arose, leading to the displacement and marginalization of indigenous peoples. The consequences of these actions would reverberate for generations to come.

Economically, the Louisiana Purchase provided the United States with valuable resources and fertile land, contributing to the nation's rapid growth and development. It also solidified the United States' position as an emerging global power, setting the stage for future territorial expansion and the pursuit of Manifest Destiny.

In conclusion, the Louisiana Purchase was a pivotal moment in American history. It not only secured vital access to the Mississippi River and the port of New Orleans but also opened up vast opportunities for westward expansion and economic growth. While it raised questions about the constitutionality of such a large acquisition, its benefits far outweighed any concerns. The Louisiana Purchase remains a testament to the vision and ambition of the Founding Fathers, who shaped the destiny of the United States through their bold actions and strategic decisions.

5.4 The War of 1812 and its Consequences

The War of 1812, often referred to as America's "Second War of Independence," was a conflict between the United States and Great Britain that lasted from 1812 to 1815. This war had significant consequences for both nations and played a crucial role in shaping the future of the United States.

Background and Causes of the War

Tensions between the United States and Great Britain had been simmering for years leading up to the War of 1812. One of the primary causes was the British practice of impressment, which involved the forced recruitment of American sailors into the British Navy. This violated American sovereignty and led to growing resentment among the American people.

Additionally, the British were providing support to Native American tribes in the Northwest Territory, who were resisting American expansion into their lands. This further strained relations between the two nations.

The Course of the War

The war began with a series of American military failures, including the unsuccessful invasion of Canada. However, the American Navy achieved several notable victories, most notably the USS Constitution's defeat of the HMS Guerriere, earning it the nickname "Old Ironsides."

In 1814, the British launched a major offensive, capturing Washington, D.C., and burning down many government buildings, including the White House. However, their advance was halted at the Battle of Baltimore, where American forces successfully defended Fort McHenry, inspiring Francis Scott Key to write "The Star-Spangled Banner."

The war reached its climax with the Battle of New Orleans in January 1815. Under the leadership of General Andrew Jackson, American forces achieved a decisive victory over the British, despite being outnumbered. This victory, although occurring after the signing of the Treaty of Ghent, boosted American morale and became a symbol of American resilience and military prowess.

Consequences of the War

The War of 1812 had several significant consequences for both the United States and Great Britain.

1. National Identity and Unity

The war played a crucial role in solidifying American national identity and unity. The successful defense of Fort McHenry and the victory at the Battle of New Orleans instilled a sense of pride and patriotism among Americans. The war also marked the end of British interference in American affairs and further established the United States as a sovereign nation.

2. Native American Relations

The war had a profound impact on Native American tribes. Many tribes had allied with the British, hoping to halt American expansion into their territories. However, the defeat of the British weakened their position, and the subsequent Treaty of Ghent did not address Native American concerns. This led to increased pressure on Native American lands and the implementation of policies that would ultimately result in the forced removal of tribes from their ancestral lands.

3. International Standing

The War of 1812 had significant implications for America's international standing. Despite not achieving all of its objectives, the United States demonstrated its ability to defend itself against a major world power. This newfound confidence and military reputation helped to solidify America's position as a respected nation on the global stage.

4. Economic Consequences

The war had both positive and negative economic consequences for the United States. On one hand, the conflict stimulated domestic manufacturing as American industries had to produce goods that were previously imported from Britain. This helped to foster economic independence and growth.

On the other hand, the war disrupted trade and caused economic hardships for many Americans, particularly those involved in maritime industries. The British naval blockade severely impacted American commerce, leading to financial struggles for merchants and sailors.

5. The End of the Federalist Party

The War of 1812 dealt a severe blow to the Federalist Party, which had been critical of the war and had even considered secession. The party's opposition to the conflict, seen as unpatriotic by many Americans, led to a decline in its popularity and influence. The war solidified the dominance of the Democratic-Republican Party and marked the beginning of the "Era of Good Feelings."

Legacy and Significance

The War of 1812 is often overshadowed by other conflicts in American history, such as the Revolutionary War and the Civil War. However, its consequences were far-reaching and played a crucial role in shaping the United States.

The war solidified American independence and national identity, established the United States as a respected nation on the global stage, and contributed to the westward expansion of the country. It also highlighted the importance of a strong navy and a well-trained military, leading to increased investment in defense and national security.

Furthermore, the war's impact on Native American tribes and the subsequent policies of removal and assimilation had long-lasting consequences for indigenous communities. The economic effects of the war, both positive and negative, shaped the trajectory of American industry and commerce.

In conclusion, the War of 1812 was a pivotal moment in American history. It tested the young nation's resolve and ability to defend itself against a major world power. The war's consequences, both immediate and long-term, continue to shape the United States and its place in the world.

The Founding Fathers and Native Americans

6.1 Conflicts and Treaties

The relationship between the Founding Fathers and Native Americans was complex and often marked by conflicts and treaties. As the United States expanded westward, the Native American tribes found themselves caught in the crossfire of territorial disputes and the relentless push for land by European settlers. This section explores the conflicts that arose between the Founding Fathers and Native Americans, as well as the treaties that were negotiated in an attempt to establish peace and coexistence.

The early interactions between the Founding Fathers and Native Americans were characterized by a mixture of cooperation and conflict. Some of the Founding Fathers, such as Thomas Jefferson, believed in the assimilation of Native Americans into American society. Jefferson saw Native Americans as "savages" who could be "civilized" through education and exposure to European culture. He proposed a policy of assimilation that aimed to transform Native Americans into farmers and craftsmen, adopting the ways of the white settlers.

However, not all Founding Fathers shared Jefferson's views. Some, like George Washington, recognized the sovereignty of Native American tribes and sought to establish peaceful relations through treaties. Washington believed that it was essential to negotiate with Native American leaders and respect their rights to their ancestral lands. He saw the Native American tribes as independent nations with whom the United States should engage in diplomatic relations.

Despite these efforts, conflicts between Native Americans and the United States were inevitable. The westward expansion of American settlers encroached upon Native American territories, leading to tensions and violence. Native American tribes, such as the Shawnee and the Creek, resisted the encroachment and fought to defend their lands and way of life. The United States government, under the leadership of the Founding Fathers, responded with military force to suppress these uprisings and protect American settlers.

One of the most significant conflicts between the Founding Fathers and Native Americans was the Northwest Indian War, also known as Little Turtle's War. This conflict, which took place between 1785 and 1795, pitted the United States against a confederation of Native American tribes led by Chief Little Turtle of the Miami tribe. The Native American forces achieved several victories against the United States Army, but ultimately, they were defeated at the Battle of Fallen Timbers in 1794. The Treaty of Greenville, signed in 1795, marked the end of the war and resulted in the cession of Native American lands in the Northwest Territory to the United States.

Treaties played a crucial role in the relationship between the Founding Fathers and Native Americans. These agreements were intended to establish peace, define boundaries, and regulate trade between the United States and Native American tribes. However, the treaties were often unequal and heavily favored the United States. Native American tribes were forced to cede vast amounts of land in exchange for meager compensation or promises of protection.

One of the most infamous treaties was the Indian Removal Act of 1830, signed into law by President Andrew Jackson. This act authorized the forced removal of Native American tribes from their ancestral lands in the southeastern United States to territories west of the Mississippi River. The Trail of Tears, which refers to the forced relocation of the Cherokee Nation, resulted in the deaths of thousands of Native Americans due to disease, starvation, and exposure.

The conflicts and treaties between the Founding Fathers and Native Americans had a lasting impact on Native American communities. The loss of land, resources, and cultural heritage had devastating consequences for Native American tribes. Many tribes were displaced and forced to adapt to unfamiliar environments, leading to the erosion of their traditional way of life.

In conclusion, the relationship between the Founding Fathers and Native Americans was marked by conflicts and treaties. While some Founding Fathers advocated for assimilation and peaceful coexistence, others pursued policies of territorial expansion and forced removal. The conflicts and treaties that arose from these interactions had profound and lasting consequences for

Native American tribes, shaping their history and the legacy of the Founding Fathers.

6.2 Assimilation and Removal Policies

The relationship between the Founding Fathers and Native Americans was complex and often marked by conflict. As the United States expanded westward, the issue of how to deal with Native American tribes became increasingly pressing. The Founding Fathers grappled with the question of how to assimilate or remove Native Americans from their ancestral lands, leading to the implementation of assimilation and removal policies.

Assimilation Policies

One approach advocated by some Founding Fathers was the assimilation of Native Americans into Euro-American society. This idea was rooted in the belief that Native Americans could be "civilized" by adopting European customs, language, and Christianity. Thomas Jefferson, in particular, held this view and believed that Native Americans could become farmers and adopt a sedentary lifestyle.

Jefferson's vision of assimilation was reflected in his policies as President. In 1803, he established the Office of Indian Affairs, which aimed to promote agriculture and education among Native American tribes. Jefferson believed that by adopting an agrarian lifestyle, Native Americans would become self-sufficient and integrate into American society.

Another proponent of assimilation was Henry Knox, the first Secretary of War under President George Washington. Knox proposed a plan known as the "Plan of Civilization" in 1789, which aimed to assimilate Native Americans by providing them with education, agricultural tools, and assistance in establishing farms. The plan, however, faced significant challenges and was not fully implemented.

Despite these efforts, assimilation policies often failed to achieve their intended goals. Native American tribes had their own distinct cultures, languages, and traditions, which they were reluctant to abandon. Additionally, the rapid expansion of white settlers into Native American territories often led to conflicts and further strained relations.

Removal Policies

As the United States expanded westward, the issue of Native American land ownership became increasingly contentious. Many white settlers desired access to fertile lands occupied by Native American tribes. This led to the formulation and implementation of removal policies, which aimed to relocate Native Americans to designated territories.

The Indian Removal Act of 1830, signed into law by President Andrew Jackson, was a significant milestone in the implementation of removal policies. The act authorized the federal government to negotiate treaties with Native American tribes, exchanging their ancestral lands for lands in the West. This policy was justified by the belief that removing Native Americans from their lands would protect them from further conflicts with white settlers.

One of the most infamous examples of removal was the forced relocation of the Cherokee Nation, known as the Trail of Tears. In 1838, thousands of Cherokee people were forcibly removed from their lands in Georgia and forced to march westward to present-day Oklahoma. The journey was arduous, and thousands of Cherokee died due to exposure, disease, and starvation.

The removal policies implemented by the United States government were met with resistance from Native American tribes. Some tribes, such as the Cherokee, attempted to fight the removal through legal means. They challenged the constitutionality of the Indian Removal Act in court but were ultimately unsuccessful.

The implementation of removal policies had devastating consequences for Native American tribes. They were uprooted from their ancestral lands, which held deep cultural and spiritual significance. The forced relocation disrupted their social structures, economies, and traditional ways of life. Many tribes suffered immense loss of life and cultural heritage as a result of these policies.

Legacy and Reckoning

The assimilation and removal policies pursued by the Founding Fathers had a profound and lasting impact on Native American communities. The forced relocation and loss of ancestral lands had devastating consequences that continue to be felt today. Native American tribes continue to grapple with the legacy of these policies, as they strive to preserve their cultural heritage and reclaim their rights.

In recent years, there has been a growing recognition of the injustices inflicted upon Native Americans by the United States government. Efforts are being made to address historical grievances and promote greater understanding and reconciliation. The establishment of tribal sovereignty and the recognition of Native American rights have been important steps towards rectifying past injustices.

The assimilation and removal policies pursued by the Founding Fathers reflect the complexities and contradictions of the early American nation-building process. While the Founding Fathers laid the foundation for a democratic and inclusive society, their actions towards Native Americans reveal the darker side of American history. Understanding and acknowledging this history is crucial for a more comprehensive and accurate understanding of the Founding Fathers and the nation they helped create.

6.3 Native American Resistance

Throughout the history of the United States, Native American tribes have faced numerous challenges and injustices at the hands of European settlers and the American government. As the young nation expanded westward, conflicts between Native Americans and the new settlers became inevitable. Native American resistance to this encroachment on their lands and way of life was a natural response to protect their sovereignty and cultural heritage.

Native American resistance took various forms, ranging from diplomatic negotiations to armed conflicts. Many tribes initially sought peaceful coexistence with the newcomers, but as their lands were taken and their rights violated, they were left with no choice but to defend themselves. This section explores the different aspects of Native American resistance and the lasting impact it had on their communities.

Early Conflicts and Diplomacy

In the early years of European colonization, Native American tribes often engaged in diplomatic negotiations with the settlers. They sought to establish alliances and maintain their autonomy in the face of increasing encroachment. Tribes such as the Iroquois Confederacy and the Cherokee Nation engaged in treaties and agreements with the British and later the American government to protect their lands and secure their rights.

However, as the United States expanded westward, conflicts between Native Americans and settlers escalated. The Indian Removal Act of 1830, signed into law by President Andrew Jackson, forced the relocation of numerous tribes from their ancestral lands to designated Indian Territory in present-day Oklahoma. This policy of forced removal led to the infamous Trail of Tears, resulting in the deaths of thousands of Native Americans.

Armed Resistance and Wars

Native American tribes also engaged in armed resistance to protect their lands and way of life. One notable example is the resistance led by the Shawnee chief Tecumseh and his brother Tenskwatawa, also known as the Prophet. They sought to unite various tribes in the Northwest Territory to resist American expansion. Their efforts culminated in the Battle of Tippecanoe in 1811, where they were ultimately defeated by American forces led by General William Henry Harrison.

Another significant conflict was the Sioux Wars, which occurred in the late 19th century. The Sioux, led by leaders such as Sitting Bull and Crazy Horse, fiercely resisted the encroachment of settlers and the U.S. government's attempts to force them onto reservations. The most famous battle of this conflict was the Battle of Little Bighorn in 1876, where Native American forces achieved a significant victory over General George Custer and his troops.

Cultural Preservation and Revitalization

In addition to armed resistance, Native American tribes also focused on preserving and revitalizing their cultural heritage. Efforts were made to maintain traditional practices, languages, and spiritual beliefs in the face of assimilation policies imposed by the American government. Native American leaders, such as the Nez Perce Chief Joseph, advocated for the preservation of their way of life and the rights of their people.

Despite the challenges they faced, Native American tribes have managed to maintain their cultural identity and traditions. Today, many tribes continue to fight for their rights, including land and water rights, recognition, and self-governance. Native American resistance has played a crucial role in shaping the ongoing struggle for indigenous rights and sovereignty in the United States.

The Lasting Impact on Native American Communities

The consequences of Native American resistance are still felt today. The loss of ancestral lands, forced relocation, and the devastating impact of diseases brought by European settlers have had long-lasting effects on Native American communities. Many tribes continue to face economic and social challenges resulting from historical injustices.

Furthermore, the forced assimilation policies implemented by the American government, such as the Indian boarding school system, aimed to eradicate Native American culture and languages. These policies had a profound impact on Native American communities, leading to the loss of cultural knowledge and the disruption of intergenerational transmission of traditions.

In recent years, there has been a growing recognition of the importance of Native American history and the need to address past injustices. Efforts are being made to promote cultural revitalization, preserve sacred sites, and support tribal self-governance. The ongoing dialogue between Native American tribes and the U.S. government seeks to address the historical grievances and work towards a more equitable future.

Native American resistance stands as a testament to the resilience and strength of indigenous peoples in the face of adversity. Their struggles and triumphs have contributed to the rich tapestry of American history and serve as a reminder of the importance of respecting and honoring the rights and sovereignty of Native American tribes.

6.4 The Lasting Impact on Native American Communities

The interaction between the Founding Fathers and Native American communities is a complex and often tragic chapter in American history. The policies and actions of the early American government had a lasting impact on Native American communities, shaping their lives and the trajectory of their cultures for generations to come.

From the earliest days of European colonization, Native American tribes faced significant challenges as they navigated the arrival of newcomers on their lands. The Founding Fathers, while recognizing the sovereignty of Native nations in theory, often failed to uphold these principles in practice. Conflicts and treaties became a common occurrence as the United States expanded westward, leading to the displacement and dispossession of Native peoples.

Conflicts and Treaties

The Founding Fathers inherited a complex web of relationships between Native American tribes and European powers. As the United States emerged as a new nation, it sought to establish its authority over Native lands. This often led to conflicts, as both sides fought for control and resources.

One notable example is the Northwest Indian War, which took place from 1785 to 1795. This conflict arose as Native tribes, led by leaders such as Little Turtle and Blue Jacket, resisted American expansion into the Northwest Territory. The United States eventually emerged victorious, but not without significant loss of life on both sides.

In an attempt to establish peaceful relations, the United States also entered into numerous treaties with Native American tribes. These treaties aimed to define boundaries, establish trade relationships, and secure peace. However, many of these agreements were marked by unequal power dynamics and broken promises.

Assimilation and Removal Policies

As the United States expanded westward, the government implemented policies aimed at assimilating Native American tribes into American society or removing them from their ancestral lands. These policies were driven by a combination of cultural superiority, economic interests, and the desire for territorial expansion.

One of the most infamous examples of assimilation policies was the Indian Removal Act of 1830, signed into law by President Andrew Jackson. This act authorized the forced removal of Native American tribes from their ancestral lands in the southeastern United States to territories west of the Mississippi River. The Trail of Tears, which resulted from the implementation of this act, led to the death and suffering of thousands of Native Americans.

Native American Resistance

Despite the challenges they faced, Native American tribes demonstrated resilience and resistance against the encroachment of the United States. Leaders such as Tecumseh, Sitting Bull, and Geronimo emerged as symbols of Native American resistance, fighting to protect their lands, cultures, and ways of life.

The Battle of Little Bighorn in 1876, where Lakota, Cheyenne, and Arapaho warriors defeated General George Custer and his troops, stands as a testament to the determination and military prowess of Native American tribes. However, these victories were often short-lived, as the United States continued to exert its dominance through military force and broken treaties.

The Lasting Impact on Native American Communities

The policies and actions of the Founding Fathers had a profound and lasting impact on Native American communities. The forced removal of tribes from their ancestral lands disrupted social structures, led to the loss of cultural practices, and caused immense suffering.

The establishment of reservations, while intended to provide a semblance of autonomy, often resulted in poverty, limited access to resources, and the erosion of traditional ways of life. Native American communities continue to face significant challenges, including high rates of poverty, unemployment, and health disparities.

Furthermore, the legacy of the Founding Fathers' actions continues to shape the relationship between the United States government and Native American tribes. Efforts to address historical injustices, promote tribal sovereignty, and foster economic development on reservations are ongoing, but progress has been slow and uneven.

In recent years, there has been a growing recognition of the need to acknowledge and address the historical and ongoing injustices faced by Native American communities. Efforts to promote cultural preservation, strengthen tribal governments, and improve access to education and healthcare are steps towards healing the wounds of the past.

The lasting impact on Native American communities serves as a reminder of the complex and often painful history of the United States. It highlights the need for continued dialogue, understanding, and reconciliation as the nation strives to live up to its ideals of liberty, justice, and equality for all.

The Founding Fathers and Women's Rights

85

7.1 The Role of Women in the Founding Era

The founding era of the United States was a time of great change and transformation. It was a period when the ideals of liberty, equality, and justice were being debated and defined. While the founding fathers played a significant role in shaping the nation, it is important to recognize that women also played a crucial part in the development of the United States.

During the late 18th century, women's roles in society were largely confined to the domestic sphere. They were expected to be wives, mothers, and caretakers of the household. However, despite these limitations, many women found ways to contribute to the founding of the nation.

One of the most notable women of the founding era was Abigail Adams, the wife of John Adams, who would later become the second President of the United States. Abigail Adams was a strong advocate for women's rights and equality. In her letters to her husband, she urged him to "remember the ladies" and to consider their rights when drafting the new laws of the nation. Although her pleas were not immediately heeded, her words laid the foundation for future discussions on women's rights.

Another influential woman of the founding era was Mercy Otis Warren. Warren was a playwright and political writer who used her pen to advocate for independence and to criticize British rule. Her plays and writings were widely read and helped to shape public opinion during the Revolutionary War. Warren's work not only contributed to the cause of independence but also challenged traditional gender roles by demonstrating that women were capable of engaging in political discourse.

In addition to these prominent figures, countless other women made significant contributions to the founding of the nation. Women like Martha Washington, the wife of George Washington, played a vital role in supporting their husbands and providing stability during times of uncertainty. They managed households, raised children, and often acted as advisors to their husbands, offering guidance and support in their decision-making.

Women also played a crucial role in the fight for independence. They participated in boycotts of British goods, organized fundraising events, and even served as spies during the Revolutionary War. Women like Deborah Sampson and Molly Pitcher disguised themselves as men and fought alongside their male counterparts on the battlefield. Their bravery and sacrifice demonstrated that women were willing to risk their lives for the cause of freedom.

Despite their contributions, women's rights were not a central focus during the founding era. The political and legal systems of the time were largely designed to exclude women from active participation in public life. Women were denied the right to vote, hold public office, or own property in their own name. However, the revolutionary ideals of liberty and equality planted the seeds for future movements advocating for women's rights.

The founding era laid the groundwork for the women's rights movement that would emerge in the 19th century. The ideas of equality and individual rights that were central to the founding of the nation provided a framework for women to demand their own rights and freedoms. The Seneca Falls Convention of 1848 marked a turning point in the fight for women's suffrage, as women gathered to discuss their grievances and draft a Declaration of Sentiments demanding equal rights for women.

The struggle for women's rights would continue long after the founding era, but the contributions of women during this time cannot be overlooked. Their efforts helped to shape the nation and laid the foundation for future generations of women to fight for their rights. The role of women in the founding era serves as a reminder that the fight for equality is an ongoing process, and that the principles of liberty and justice must be extended to all members of society.

7.2 Early Advocates for Women's Rights

The struggle for women's rights in America has a long and complex history that dates back to the founding era. While the Founding Fathers are often celebrated for their role in establishing the principles of liberty and equality, it is important to recognize that their vision of a new nation did not initially include women as equal participants in society. However, there were early advocates for women's rights who challenged the prevailing norms and fought for greater gender equality.

One of the earliest voices for women's rights was Abigail Adams, the wife of John Adams, who would later become the second President of the United States. In a letter to her husband in 1776, Abigail Adams famously wrote, "Remember the ladies, and be more generous and favorable to them than your ancestors." She urged him to consider the rights and interests of women in the formation of the new government. While her plea did not result in immediate change, it marked an important early call for women's rights.

Another influential figure in the early advocacy for women's rights was Judith Sargent Murray. In 1779, Murray published an essay titled "On the Equality of the Sexes," in which she argued that women were capable of intellectual and moral achievements equal to those of men. Murray challenged the prevailing belief that women were inherently inferior to men and called for greater educational opportunities for women. Her essay was one of the earliest feminist works in America and laid the groundwork for future discussions on women's rights.

The early 19th century saw the emergence of a more organized movement for women's rights. One of the key figures during this period was Elizabeth Cady Stanton. Stanton played a pivotal role in organizing the Seneca Falls Convention in 1848, which is often considered the birthplace of the women's rights movement in the United States. At the convention, Stanton and other women activists drafted the Declaration of Sentiments, which demanded equal rights for women, including the right to vote. The convention marked a significant turning point in the fight for women's rights and set the stage for future activism.

Another prominent advocate for women's rights during this time was Lucretia Mott. Mott was a Quaker minister and abolitionist who dedicated her life to fighting for social reform. She played a crucial role in organizing the Seneca Falls Convention and was one of the signatories of the Declaration of Sentiments. Mott's commitment to women's rights and her tireless efforts to challenge gender inequality made her a respected leader in the movement.

The early advocates for women's rights faced significant opposition and criticism. Many people, including some women, believed that women's proper place was in the domestic sphere and that they were not suited for public life or political participation. However, the early activists persisted in their fight for equality.

The Seneca Falls Convention and the Declaration of Sentiments sparked a wave of activism and laid the foundation for future generations of women's rights advocates. The suffrage movement gained momentum in the late 19th and early 20th centuries, leading to the eventual passage of the 19th Amendment in 1920, which granted women the right to vote.

The early advocates for women's rights played a crucial role in challenging the prevailing gender norms and paving the way for greater gender equality. Their efforts laid the foundation for future generations of women's rights activists and set the stage for the ongoing struggle for gender equality in America.

While the Founding Fathers may not have initially included women in their vision of a new nation, the early advocates for women's rights fought tirelessly to ensure that women's voices were heard and their rights were recognized. Their contributions to the fight for gender equality should not be overlooked or forgotten. The ongoing struggle for women's rights serves as a reminder that progress is not always immediate or linear, but it is through the dedication and perseverance of individuals that change is achieved.

7.3 The Seneca Falls Convention

The Seneca Falls Convention, held in Seneca Falls, New York, in July 1848, was a pivotal event in the history of women's rights and the fight for gender equality in the United States. It marked the beginning of the organized women's suffrage movement and laid the foundation for future activism and advocacy.

The Context of the Convention

In the early 19th century, women in the United States faced significant legal and social restrictions. They were denied basic rights, including the right to vote, own property, and participate in public life. Inspired by the ideals of the American Revolution and the fight for abolition, a growing number of women began to question their subordinate status and demand equal rights.

The Visionaries Behind the Convention

The Seneca Falls Convention was organized by a group of remarkable women, including Elizabeth Cady Stanton, Lucretia Mott, Martha Coffin Wright, Mary Ann McClintock, and Jane Hunt. These women were influenced by the abolitionist movement and the principles of the Declaration of Independence, which declared that "all men are created equal." They believed that these principles should apply to women as well.

The Declaration of Sentiments

At the Seneca Falls Convention, the attendees drafted a document known as the Declaration of Sentiments, which was modeled after the Declaration of Independence. The Declaration of Sentiments outlined the grievances and demands of women, asserting that women were entitled to the same rights and privileges as men. It called for women's suffrage, access to education, and equal opportunities in employment and property ownership.

The Significance of the Convention

The Seneca Falls Convention was a groundbreaking event that brought the issue of women's rights into the public consciousness. It was the first women's rights convention in the United States and marked the beginning of a long and arduous struggle for gender equality. The convention received significant media coverage, which helped to spread its message and inspire other women to join the cause.

The Legacy of the Seneca Falls Convention

While the immediate impact of the Seneca Falls Convention was limited, it laid the groundwork for future activism and advocacy. The Declaration of Sentiments served as a blueprint for the women's suffrage movement, which gained momentum in the following decades. The convention also established a network of women activists who would continue to fight for women's rights and pave the way for future generations.

Challenges and Opposition

The Seneca Falls Convention faced significant opposition and criticism. Many people, including some women, believed that women's rights were a threat to the established social order. The convention was met with ridicule and hostility in some quarters, and its demands were dismissed as radical and unrealistic. However, the women who attended the convention remained steadfast in their commitment to the cause and continued to advocate for change.

The Long Road to Suffrage

It would take several more decades of tireless activism and advocacy before women in the United States would finally achieve the right to vote. The suffrage movement faced numerous obstacles and setbacks along the way, including opposition from conservative forces and the slow pace of legislative change. However, the spirit of the Seneca Falls Convention persisted, and women's suffrage became a central issue in the fight for civil rights.

The Impact on Future Generations

The Seneca Falls Convention and the women's suffrage movement that followed it had a profound impact on future generations. The convention inspired women across the country to organize and demand their rights. It paved the way for the formation of women's suffrage organizations, such as the National American Woman Suffrage Association, and the eventual passage of the 19th Amendment to the U.S. Constitution in 1920, which granted women the right to vote.

Continuing the Struggle for Gender Equality

While the Seneca Falls Convention was a significant milestone in the fight for gender equality, it was just the beginning of a long and ongoing struggle. Even after gaining the right to vote, women continued to face discrimination and inequality in various aspects of their lives. The convention serves as a reminder that the fight for gender equality is not a one-time event but a continuous effort that requires the dedication and perseverance of future generations.

Conclusion

The Seneca Falls Convention was a pivotal moment in the history of women's rights in the United States. It brought together visionary women who dared to challenge the status quo and demand equal rights for themselves and future generations. The convention laid the foundation for the women's suffrage movement and inspired countless women to join the fight for gender equality. While the struggle for women's rights continues, the Seneca Falls Convention remains a symbol of courage, determination, and the power of collective action.

7.4 The Ongoing Struggle for Gender Equality

Throughout history, the struggle for gender equality has been a constant battle, and the Founding Fathers of the United States were no exception to this ongoing fight. While they laid the foundation for a new nation based on principles of liberty and equality, their vision did not initially extend to women's rights. However, the seeds of change were sown during the founding era, and the fight for gender equality would continue long after their time.

The Role of Women in the Founding Era

During the founding era, women played vital roles in the development of the new nation. They were active participants in the Revolutionary War, providing support to the soldiers by working as nurses, spies, and even soldiers themselves. Women also took on responsibilities at home, managing households, farms, and businesses while their husbands were away at war. Despite their contributions, women were largely excluded from the political and legal spheres.

Early Advocates for Women's Rights

In the years following the Revolutionary War, a few brave women began to speak out against the inequality they faced. One of the earliest advocates for women's rights was Abigail Adams, the wife of John Adams. In a letter to her husband in 1776, she famously wrote, "Remember the ladies, and be more generous and favorable to them than your ancestors." Her words highlighted the need for women to have a voice in the new government.

Another influential figure was Judith Sargent Murray, who wrote essays advocating for women's education and equality. In her 1790 essay, "On the Equality of the Sexes," Murray argued that women were just as capable as men and should be given the same opportunities for education and self-improvement.

The Seneca Falls Convention

The fight for gender equality gained significant momentum in the mid-19th century with the Seneca Falls Convention. Held in 1848 in Seneca Falls, New York, this convention marked the beginning of the organized women's rights movement in the United States. Led by prominent activists such as Elizabeth Cady Stanton and Lucretia Mott, the convention issued the Declaration of Sentiments, which demanded equal rights for women, including the right to vote.

The Seneca Falls Convention was a pivotal moment in the struggle for gender equality, as it brought national attention to the cause and inspired future generations of activists. However, it would take several more decades of tireless advocacy and activism before significant progress was made.

The Ongoing Struggle

Despite the efforts of early advocates and the suffrage movement, progress towards gender equality was slow. It wasn't until 1920 that the 19th Amendment was ratified, granting women the right to vote. This milestone achievement marked a significant victory for the women's rights movement, but it was only the beginning of a long journey towards full equality.

In the decades that followed, women continued to fight for equal rights in various areas, including education, employment, and reproductive rights. The feminist movement of the 1960s and 1970s brought renewed energy to the cause, leading to landmark legislation such as the Equal Pay Act of 1963 and the Roe v. Wade Supreme Court decision in 1973.

However, even with these advancements, gender inequality persists in many aspects of society. Women still face challenges in the workplace, including wage disparities and underrepresentation in leadership positions. Issues such as sexual harassment and violence against women remain prevalent, highlighting the ongoing need for change.

The Path Forward

The ongoing struggle for gender equality requires continued activism, awareness, and policy changes. It is essential to challenge societal norms and stereotypes that perpetuate gender inequality. Education plays a crucial role in promoting gender equality, as it helps to dismantle biases and empower individuals to advocate for change.

Supporting organizations and initiatives that promote women's rights and gender equality is another way to contribute to the ongoing struggle. By amplifying women's voices, advocating for equal opportunities, and working towards dismantling systemic barriers, progress can be made.

The Founding Fathers may not have initially envisioned a society where women had equal rights, but their principles of liberty and equality laid the groundwork for future generations to continue the fight. The ongoing struggle for gender equality is a testament to the enduring legacy of the Founding Fathers and their vision of a more perfect union.

The Founding Fathers and Religious Freedom

8.1 Religion in the Early Republic

Religion played a significant role in the early years of the United States, as the Founding Fathers grappled with the question of how to balance religious freedom with the need for a stable and cohesive society. The religious landscape of the early republic was diverse, with various Christian denominations, as well as Jewish and other non-Christian communities, coexisting and sometimes clashing in their beliefs and practices.

The Influence of Christianity

Christianity, particularly Protestantism, was the dominant religious tradition in the early republic. Many of the Founding Fathers were themselves Christians, and their religious beliefs influenced their views on governance and individual rights. However, it is important to note that the Founders held a range of religious beliefs, from devout Christianity to more skeptical or deistic perspectives.

The influence of Christianity can be seen in the language and ideas expressed in the founding documents of the United States. For example, the Declaration of Independence references a "Creator" and asserts that individuals are endowed with "certain unalienable Rights." These ideas reflect a belief in natural law and the inherent worth and dignity of every individual, concepts that have deep roots in Christian thought.

Separation of Church and State

Despite the influence of Christianity, the Founding Fathers were also committed to the principle of religious freedom and the separation of church and state. They sought to create a government that would not establish an official religion or interfere with the free exercise of religion by individuals.

Thomas Jefferson, one of the key architects of the early republic, famously wrote in a letter to the Danbury Baptist Association in 1802 that there should be a "wall of separation between church and state." This phrase has been widely interpreted as expressing the Founders' intent to keep religion and government separate, ensuring that no religious group would receive preferential treatment or face discrimination.

Religious Diversity and Tolerance

The early republic was marked by religious diversity and a growing spirit of religious tolerance. In addition to various Christian denominations, there were also Jewish communities, as well as smaller groups such as Quakers, Baptists, and Methodists. These diverse religious communities often coexisted peacefully, with individuals freely practicing their faith.

One notable example of religious tolerance in the early republic was the state of Rhode Island. Founded by Roger Williams, a Baptist minister who was expelled from the Massachusetts Bay Colony for his religious beliefs, Rhode Island became a haven for religious dissenters. The state's charter explicitly guaranteed religious freedom and served as a model for the later inclusion of religious freedom in the First Amendment to the United States Constitution.

Challenges and Controversies

While the Founding Fathers sought to protect religious freedom, there were still challenges and controversies surrounding religion in the early republic. One such controversy was the issue of religious tests for holding public office. Some states, such as Maryland and South Carolina, required individuals to be Christians in order to hold certain positions of power. These requirements were eventually abolished, as the principle of religious freedom gained wider acceptance.

Another challenge was the question of how to handle religious practices that were seen as incompatible with the values of the new nation. For example, the practice of polygamy among some Mormon communities in the early 19th century raised concerns among some Americans. Ultimately, the federal government took action against polygamy, leading to the eventual abandonment of the practice by the mainstream Mormon Church.

The Legacy of Religious Freedom

The early republic's commitment to religious freedom and the separation of church and state laid the foundation for the religious landscape of the United States today. The First Amendment to the United States Constitution, ratified in 1791, guarantees the free exercise of religion and prohibits the establishment of an official religion.

Over the years, the interpretation and application of these principles have evolved through court cases and legal debates. The Supreme Court has grappled with questions such as the extent to which religious practices can be exempt from generally applicable laws and the boundaries of religious expression in public spaces. These ongoing debates reflect the complex and ever-changing nature of religious freedom in the United States.

In conclusion, religion played a significant role in the early republic, with Christianity being the dominant religious tradition. However, the Founding Fathers were committed to the principles of religious freedom and the separation of church and state. The early republic was marked by religious diversity and a growing spirit of tolerance, although challenges and controversies surrounding religion also emerged. The legacy of religious freedom established by the Founding Fathers continues to shape the religious landscape of the United States today.

8.2 The Separation of Church and State

The concept of the separation of church and state is a fundamental principle that has shaped the United States since its inception. It is a cornerstone of American democracy and a testament to the foresight and wisdom of the Founding Fathers. In this section, we will explore the origins of this principle, its significance in the early republic, and its lasting impact on religious freedom in America.

Origins of the Principle

The idea of separating church and state can be traced back to the Enlightenment era, a period of intellectual and philosophical awakening in Europe during the 17th and 18th centuries. Influenced by thinkers such as John Locke and Thomas Paine, the Founding Fathers embraced the concept of religious freedom and sought to establish a government that would not favor any particular religion.

The roots of the separation of church and state can also be found in the religious diversity of the American colonies. Many of the early settlers came to America seeking religious freedom, escaping persecution in their homelands. This experience shaped their understanding of the importance of religious liberty and the need to prevent the government from interfering in matters of faith.

The First Amendment

The principle of the separation of church and state was enshrined in the First Amendment to the United States Constitution, which was ratified in 1791. The First Amendment states, "Congress shall make no law respecting an establishment of religion, or prohibiting the free exercise thereof." This language reflects the Founding Fathers' commitment to religious freedom and their desire to prevent the government from establishing an official religion or interfering with the practice of religion.

The First Amendment not only protects the rights of individuals to worship as they choose but also ensures that the government remains neutral in matters of religion. It prohibits the government from favoring one religion over another or imposing religious beliefs on its citizens. This principle has been upheld by the courts and has become a cornerstone of American jurisprudence.

Early Challenges and Interpretations

Despite the clear language of the First Amendment, the interpretation and application of the principle of the separation of church and state have been the subject of ongoing debate and controversy throughout American history. Different interpretations have emerged, ranging from strict separationism to accommodationism.

One of the earliest challenges to the principle came in the form of government support for religious institutions. In the early years of the republic, some states continued to provide financial support to churches, leading to concerns about the establishment of a state religion. These practices were eventually challenged and struck down by the courts, reinforcing the principle of separation.

Another area of contention has been the role of religion in public life. While the First Amendment prohibits the government from promoting or endorsing a particular religion, it does not prohibit religious expression in the public sphere. This has led to debates over issues such as prayer in schools, religious displays on public property, and the inclusion of religious symbols in government ceremonies. Courts have grappled with striking a balance between protecting religious freedom and preventing government endorsement of religion.

Evolving Understanding and Challenges

Over time, the understanding of the separation of church and state has evolved and faced new challenges. The Supreme Court has played a crucial role in shaping the interpretation of the First Amendment and defining the boundaries between religion and government.

In the landmark case of Everson v. Board of Education (1947), the Supreme Court articulated the concept of the "wall of separation" between church and state. This metaphorical wall represents the idea that there should be a clear and distinct separation between religious institutions and government entities. It has since become a widely recognized symbol of the principle of the separation of church and state.

In recent years, new challenges have emerged, such as the intersection of religious freedom and anti-discrimination laws. Cases involving businesses refusing services based on religious beliefs, such as the Masterpiece Cakeshop case, have raised complex questions about the balance between religious liberty and equal protection under the law.

The Legacy of Religious Freedom

The principle of the separation of church and state has had a profound impact on religious freedom in America. It has allowed for the flourishing of diverse religious beliefs and practices, ensuring that individuals are free to worship according to their conscience without fear of government interference or persecution.

The United States has become a haven for religious minorities, providing a safe space for individuals of all faiths to practice their religion freely. This commitment to religious freedom has also influenced other nations around the world, inspiring movements for religious liberty and serving as a model for democratic governance.

While challenges and debates continue to shape the understanding and application of the separation of church and state, the principle remains a vital part of the American identity. It reflects the Founding Fathers' vision of a nation that respects and protects the rights of individuals to worship—or not worship—as they choose. The ongoing struggle to strike the right balance between religious freedom and the role of government ensures that the principle of the separation of church and state remains a dynamic and evolving aspect of American democracy.

8.3 Religious Diversity and Tolerance

Religious diversity and tolerance were important principles that the Founding Fathers sought to uphold in the formation of the United States. As they established a new nation, they recognized the need to protect the rights and freedoms of individuals to practice their own religious beliefs without fear of persecution or discrimination. This section explores the Founding Fathers' views on religious diversity, their efforts to promote religious tolerance, and the lasting legacy of these principles in American society.

The Founders' Views on Religious Diversity

The Founding Fathers held a range of religious beliefs, including various Christian denominations, Deism, and skepticism. They were influenced by the Enlightenment ideals of reason, individual liberty, and religious freedom. Many of them believed that religious diversity was essential for a thriving society and that the government should not favor any particular religion.

Thomas Jefferson, a key figure in the drafting of the Declaration of Independence, was a strong advocate for religious freedom. In his Virginia Statute for Religious Freedom, he argued that individuals should be free to choose their own religious beliefs and that the government should not interfere in matters of conscience. This statute later served as a model for the First Amendment to the United States Constitution.

James Madison, often referred to as the "Father of the Constitution," shared Jefferson's views on religious freedom. He believed that the government should not establish an official religion and that individuals should be free to practice their own faith without fear of persecution. Madison played a crucial role in the drafting and ratification of the First Amendment, which guarantees the freedom of religion.

Efforts to Promote Religious Tolerance

The Founding Fathers took concrete steps to promote religious tolerance and protect the rights of religious minorities. One of the most significant examples of their commitment to religious freedom was the inclusion of the First Amendment in the Bill of Rights. This amendment prohibits the government from establishing a religion and guarantees the free exercise of religion.

Additionally, the Founding Fathers sought to ensure that individuals of all religious backgrounds could participate fully in public life. They rejected religious tests for public office, which had been common in colonial America. This meant that individuals did not have to adhere to a specific religious belief to hold positions of power or influence in the new government.

The Founders also recognized the importance of religious diversity in shaping the moral fabric of the nation. They believed that a society with a variety of religious perspectives would foster a more tolerant and inclusive society. This belief was reflected in their writings and speeches, where they often emphasized the value of religious pluralism.

Challenges and Controversies

Despite their efforts to promote religious tolerance, the Founding Fathers faced challenges and controversies in implementing these principles. Some individuals and groups held deeply entrenched religious beliefs that clashed with the idea of religious diversity. There were instances of discrimination and persecution against religious minorities, particularly in the early years of the nation.

One notable controversy was the issue of religious oaths. Some states required individuals to take religious oaths as a condition for holding public office. This practice was seen as a violation of religious freedom by those who did not adhere to the prescribed religious beliefs. Over time, these requirements were gradually abolished, and the principle of religious freedom was more widely accepted.

Another challenge arose in the context of Native American religions. The Founding Fathers' commitment to religious freedom did not always extend to indigenous peoples. Native American religious practices were often suppressed or undermined as the United States expanded westward. This contradiction highlights the complexities and limitations of the Founders' approach to religious diversity.

The Legacy of Religious Freedom

The Founding Fathers' commitment to religious diversity and tolerance has had a lasting impact on American society. The principles they championed continue to shape the nation's understanding of religious freedom and the separation of church and state.

The First Amendment's protection of religious freedom has been upheld by the courts and has become a cornerstone of American democracy. It has allowed individuals of all faiths, as well as those with no religious affiliation, to freely practice their beliefs without fear of government interference.

Religious diversity is now a defining characteristic of American society. The United States is home to a wide range of religious traditions, including Christianity, Judaism, Islam, Hinduism, Buddhism, and many others. This diversity is celebrated and protected by laws that prohibit discrimination based on religion.

However, challenges to religious freedom still exist. Debates continue over issues such as the extent to which religious beliefs can be used to justify discrimination, the role of religion in public life, and the rights of religious minorities. These ongoing discussions reflect the complexities of balancing religious freedom with other societal interests.

In conclusion, the Founding Fathers recognized the importance of religious diversity and tolerance in the formation of the United States. They sought to protect the rights of individuals to practice their own religious beliefs without fear of persecution or discrimination. Their efforts to promote religious freedom, as enshrined in the First Amendment, have had a profound and lasting impact on American society. While challenges and controversies have arisen, the principles of religious diversity and tolerance remain fundamental to the nation's identity and continue to shape its ongoing quest for a more inclusive and equitable society.

8.4 The Legacy of Religious Freedom

Religious freedom was a fundamental principle that the Founding Fathers held dear and sought to protect in the newly formed United States of America. Their experiences with religious persecution in Europe and their desire to create a society where individuals could freely practice their faith without fear of oppression shaped their views on religious freedom. This section explores the legacy of religious freedom left by the Founding Fathers and its impact on American society.

The Founders' Vision of Religious Freedom

The Founding Fathers recognized the importance of religious freedom as a cornerstone of a just and prosperous society. They believed that individuals should have the right to worship according to their own conscience, free from government interference or coercion. This vision was reflected in the First Amendment to the United States Constitution, which states, "Congress shall make no law respecting an establishment of religion, or prohibiting the free exercise thereof."

Protecting Religious Pluralism

One of the key aspects of the Founders' vision of religious freedom was the protection of religious pluralism. They understood that America was a diverse nation, with people of various religious beliefs and practices. To ensure that all individuals could freely exercise their faith, the Founders sought to prevent the establishment of a state religion and to protect the rights of religious minorities.

Separation of Church and State

The concept of the separation of church and state was central to the Founders' understanding of religious freedom. They believed that the government should not favor or promote any particular religion, nor should it interfere in religious matters. This principle was intended to safeguard both the freedom of religion and the integrity of the government.

The Virginia Statute for Religious Freedom

One of the most significant contributions to the legacy of religious freedom by the Founding Fathers was the Virginia Statute for Religious Freedom. Drafted by Thomas Jefferson and passed by the Virginia General Assembly in 1786, this statute became a model for religious freedom protections in the United States. It declared that "no man shall be compelled to frequent or support any religious worship" and that "all men shall be free to profess, and by argument to maintain, their opinions in matters of religion."

Religious Tolerance and Acceptance

The Founding Fathers also emphasized the importance of religious tolerance and acceptance in a diverse society. They recognized that different religious beliefs and practices would coexist in America and that individuals should respect and tolerate the religious views of others. This commitment to religious tolerance helped foster a sense of unity and cooperation among the American people.

The Influence of the Founders' Religious Beliefs

While the Founding Fathers championed religious freedom, it is important to note that their personal religious beliefs varied. Some, like Thomas Jefferson and Benjamin Franklin, held more skeptical views of organized religion, while others, such as George Washington and John Adams, were more devout. Despite these differences, they all recognized the importance of protecting religious freedom for all Americans, regardless of their individual beliefs.

The Impact on American Society

The legacy of religious freedom left by the Founding Fathers has had a profound impact on American society. It has allowed for the flourishing of diverse religious communities and the free expression of faith. Religious institutions have played a vital role in shaping American culture, providing social services, and contributing to the moral fabric of the nation.

Challenges and Controversies

While the Founders' vision of religious freedom has been largely upheld, there have been challenges and controversies along the way. The interpretation of the separation of church and state, for example, has been the subject of ongoing debate. Issues such as prayer in public schools, religious displays on government property, and exemptions for religious organizations from certain laws have sparked legal and societal discussions about the boundaries of religious freedom.

Lessons from the Founding Fathers

The Founding Fathers' commitment to religious freedom offers valuable lessons for contemporary society. Their emphasis on protecting the rights of individuals to freely practice their faith, while respecting the rights of others, serves as a reminder of the importance of tolerance and acceptance in a diverse nation. The Founders' recognition of the potential dangers of religious establishment and their commitment to the separation of church and state provide guidance for navigating the complexities of religion in the public sphere.

In conclusion, the Founding Fathers' legacy of religious freedom has had a lasting impact on American society. Their vision of protecting religious pluralism, ensuring the separation of church and state, and promoting religious tolerance has shaped the nation's identity and allowed for the flourishing of diverse religious communities. While challenges and controversies persist, the principles established by the Founders continue to guide the ongoing pursuit of religious freedom in the United States.

The Founding Fathers and Economic Policies

9.1 The Debate over Economic Systems

The Founding Fathers of the United States were not only concerned with establishing a new government and securing individual liberties, but they also grappled with the question of economic systems. In the early years of the nation, there was a heated debate over the best economic model to adopt. This debate centered around two prominent figures: Alexander Hamilton, who advocated for a strong centralized economic system, and Thomas Jefferson, who championed an agrarian society.

At the heart of the economic debate was the question of how the new nation should organize its economy and promote economic growth. Hamilton believed that a strong central government and a robust financial system were essential for the success of the United States. He argued for a system that would encourage industrialization, trade, and commerce. Hamilton's vision was influenced by his experience as the first Secretary of the Treasury and his belief in the importance of a strong national economy.

On the other hand, Jefferson had a different perspective. He believed that the future of the United States lay in its agrarian roots. Jefferson saw agriculture as the backbone of the nation and believed that a society of independent farmers would foster self-sufficiency and preserve individual liberties. He was wary of the concentration of power in the hands of a few wealthy individuals and feared that a centralized economic system would lead to corruption and inequality.

The debate between Hamilton and Jefferson was not just an intellectual exercise; it had real consequences for the young nation. Hamilton's economic policies, which included the establishment of a national bank, the assumption of state debts, and the promotion of manufacturing, laid the foundation for a strong and prosperous economy. His policies were aimed at stimulating economic growth, attracting foreign investment, and establishing the United States as a global economic power.

Jefferson, on the other hand, advocated for a more decentralized economic system. He believed in the importance of small-scale agriculture and the virtues of self-sufficiency. Jefferson's vision was rooted in his belief in the yeoman farmer, who owned and worked his own land. He feared that the concentration of wealth and power in the hands of a few would undermine the democratic ideals upon which the nation was founded.

The debate over economic systems also had implications for the issue of slavery. Hamilton's vision of a strong centralized economy relied heavily on the institution of slavery, as the Southern states were major producers of agricultural goods such as cotton and tobacco. Jefferson, while a slaveholder himself, expressed moral qualms about the institution and believed that it was incompatible with the principles of liberty and equality.

Ultimately, Hamilton's vision of a centralized economic system prevailed in the early years of the nation. The United States embarked on a path of industrialization and economic growth, fueled by technological advancements and a growing population. The establishment of a national bank and the promotion of manufacturing helped to create a strong and stable financial system.

However, the consequences of this economic model were not without their challenges. The rapid industrialization and urbanization that accompanied Hamilton's economic policies led to social and economic inequalities. The gap between the wealthy elite and the working class widened, and the plight of workers in factories and mills became a pressing issue.

The debate over economic systems continued to shape the nation's development in the years that followed. It influenced policies on tariffs, internal improvements, and the role of government in the economy. The tension between Hamilton's vision of a centralized economy and Jefferson's agrarian ideal persisted throughout the 19th century and beyond.

In conclusion, the debate over economic systems between Alexander Hamilton and Thomas Jefferson was a fundamental part of the early years of the United States. Hamilton's vision of a strong centralized economy and Jefferson's belief in an agrarian society represented two competing visions for the future of the nation. While Hamilton's economic policies laid the foundation for a strong and prosperous economy, they also contributed to social and economic inequalities. The debate over economic systems continues to shape the nation's economic policies and serves as a reminder of the ongoing tension between centralization and decentralization in American society.

9.2 Alexander Hamilton and the Financial System

One of the most influential and controversial figures among the Founding Fathers was Alexander Hamilton. As the first Secretary of the Treasury, Hamilton played a pivotal role in shaping the economic policies of the newly formed United States. His vision and actions laid the foundation for the country's financial system and set it on a path towards economic growth and stability.

Born in the West Indies in 1755, Hamilton immigrated to the American colonies in 1772. He quickly became involved in the revolutionary cause and rose through the ranks to become one of George Washington's most trusted advisors. Hamilton's brilliance and intellect were evident from an early age, and his contributions to the nation's financial system would prove to be equally remarkable.

Hamilton's financial policies were guided by his belief in a strong central government and a robust national economy. He recognized the need for a stable currency, a well-regulated banking system, and a plan to address the massive war debt accumulated during the Revolutionary War. To achieve these goals, Hamilton proposed a series of bold and innovative measures.

One of Hamilton's most significant achievements was the establishment of the First Bank of the United States in 1791. Modeled after the Bank of England, the national bank served as a central repository for government funds, provided loans to businesses, and issued a stable national currency. The bank played a crucial role in stimulating economic growth and promoting trade within the country.

Hamilton also championed the idea of a protective tariff to encourage domestic manufacturing and protect American industries from foreign competition. He believed that a strong industrial base was essential for the nation's economic independence and security. Despite facing opposition from agrarian states, Hamilton's vision prevailed, and Congress passed the Tariff Act of 1789, which imposed duties on imported goods.

To address the issue of the war debt, Hamilton proposed a controversial plan known as the "Assumption of Debt." Under this plan, the federal government would assume the debts incurred by the states during the Revolutionary War. While this proposal faced opposition from states that had already paid off their debts, Hamilton argued that assuming the debt would strengthen the federal government's credit and establish its credibility in the eyes of foreign nations.

Hamilton's financial system also included the creation of a national mint to produce a standardized currency and the establishment of a system of taxation to generate revenue for the government. He believed that a well-funded government was necessary to maintain law and order, protect national security, and promote economic development.

Despite his many accomplishments, Hamilton's financial policies were not without controversy. His vision of a strong central government and his support for the wealthy elite led to accusations of elitism and favoritism. Hamilton's policies also faced opposition from those who believed in a more agrarian and decentralized economy, such as Thomas Jefferson.

The debate between Hamilton and Jefferson over the role of government and the direction of the economy would eventually lead to the formation of the first political parties in the United States. Hamilton's supporters, known as Federalists, advocated for a strong central government and a diversified economy, while Jefferson's followers, known as Democratic-Republicans, favored a more limited government and an agrarian society.

Despite the criticism and opposition, Hamilton's financial system laid the groundwork for the economic prosperity that would follow in the years to come. His policies helped stabilize the nation's finances, promote industrialization, and establish the United States as a global economic power.

The financial system he created provided the stability and resources necessary for the young nation to grow and thrive.

Today, Hamilton's legacy can be seen in the modern financial system of the United States. The central banking system, the use of a national currency, and the principles of economic development he championed continue to shape the country's economy. Hamilton's vision and actions as the first Secretary of the Treasury left an indelible mark on the nation's history and continue to influence economic policies to this day.

In conclusion, Alexander Hamilton's contributions to the financial system of the United States were instrumental in shaping the economic foundation of the nation. His bold and innovative policies laid the groundwork for economic growth and stability, and his vision of a strong central government and a diversified economy set the stage for the country's future prosperity. Despite facing opposition and controversy, Hamilton's financial system proved to be a triumph with far-reaching consequences for the United States.

9.3 Thomas Jefferson and Agrarianism

Thomas Jefferson, one of the most influential Founding Fathers, played a significant role in shaping the economic policies of the United States. Jefferson's vision for America was deeply rooted in agrarianism, a belief that the strength of the nation lay in its agricultural sector. This section explores Jefferson's agrarian ideals, his policies, and their impact on the American economy.

Agrarianism and Jefferson's Philosophy

Thomas Jefferson firmly believed that an agrarian society was the key to a prosperous and virtuous nation. He saw agriculture as the foundation of economic independence, self-sufficiency, and individual liberty. Jefferson believed that small, independent farmers were the backbone of society, and their virtuous and self-reliant nature would ensure the success of the nation.

Jefferson's agrarian philosophy was influenced by his experiences as a Virginia planter. He witnessed the economic and social disparities between the wealthy plantation owners and the struggling small farmers. This shaped his belief that a decentralized agrarian society would prevent the concentration of wealth and power in the hands of a few.

Agrarian Policies and Initiatives

As President, Jefferson implemented several policies to promote agrarianism and support the agricultural sector. One of his most significant achievements was the Louisiana Purchase in 1803. By acquiring vast territories in the West, Jefferson aimed to provide opportunities for small farmers to settle and cultivate new lands. This expansion of agricultural land not only aligned with his agrarian vision but also fueled westward migration and economic growth.

Jefferson also championed policies that encouraged westward expansion and agricultural development. He supported the construction of infrastructure, such as roads and canals, to facilitate trade and transportation of agricultural goods. Additionally, he advocated for the establishment of land-grant universities, like the University of Virginia, to promote agricultural education and research.

To protect American farmers from foreign competition, Jefferson implemented an embargo on trade known as the Embargo Act of 1807. This controversial policy aimed to protect American agriculture and manufacturing by restricting trade with foreign nations. However, it had unintended consequences, leading to economic hardships for American farmers and ultimately damaging the nation's economy.

Jefferson's Vision for Rural America

Jefferson's agrarian vision extended beyond economic policies. He believed that rural life fostered civic virtue and moral character. Jefferson saw the agrarian lifestyle as a means to preserve the republican values of independence, self-sufficiency, and community participation. He envisioned a nation of self-reliant farmers who actively participated in local governance and maintained a strong sense of civic duty.

To promote his vision, Jefferson advocated for the establishment of a decentralized political system. He believed that power should be vested in local governments and that the federal government should have limited authority. This philosophy was reflected in his support for states' rights and strict interpretation of the Constitution.

Impact on the American Economy

Jefferson's agrarian policies had a profound impact on the American economy, both positive and negative. On the positive side, his emphasis on westward expansion and agricultural development opened up new opportunities for settlers and farmers. The acquisition of new territories and the cultivation of fertile lands contributed to the growth of the agricultural sector and increased food production.

However, Jefferson's policies also had some negative consequences. The Embargo Act of 1807, intended to protect American farmers, resulted in a decline in trade and economic hardship for many. Additionally, Jefferson's preference for an agrarian economy limited the development of manufacturing and industrial sectors, which could have provided alternative sources of economic growth.

Despite these challenges, Jefferson's agrarian ideals left a lasting impact on American society. His vision of an independent and self-sufficient nation shaped the values and aspirations of generations to come. The agrarian legacy of Jefferson and his fellow Founding Fathers can still be seen in the importance placed on agriculture in American culture and the continued reverence for the rural way of life.

In conclusion, Thomas Jefferson's agrarian philosophy and policies played a significant role in shaping the economic landscape of the United States. His vision of an agrarian society, rooted in independence, self-sufficiency, and civic virtue, influenced policies that promoted westward expansion, agricultural development, and local governance. While his agrarian ideals had both positive and negative consequences for the American economy, they left a lasting impact on the nation's values and identity.

9.4 The Impact on American Economy

The economic policies of the Founding Fathers played a crucial role in shaping the American economy and laying the foundation for its future growth and prosperity. The debates over economic systems, led by prominent figures such as Alexander Hamilton and Thomas Jefferson, had a lasting impact on the nation's economic development.

The Debate over Economic Systems

At the heart of the Founding Fathers' economic policies was a fundamental debate over the best economic system for the new nation. On one side stood Alexander Hamilton, who advocated for a strong central government and a more industrialized economy. On the other side was Thomas Jefferson, who championed agrarianism and believed in a decentralized economy with a focus on agriculture.

Hamilton argued for a strong federal government that would promote economic growth through the establishment of a national bank, protective tariffs, and government subsidies for industries. He believed that a diverse and robust economy, with a strong manufacturing sector, would make the United States less dependent on foreign nations and enhance its economic independence.

Jefferson, on the other hand, believed that the future of the nation lay in its agrarian roots. He envisioned a society of independent farmers who would be self-sufficient and free from the corrupting influences of urbanization and industrialization. Jefferson feared that a strong central government and a focus on manufacturing would lead to the concentration of wealth and power in the hands of a few, undermining the principles of democracy.

Alexander Hamilton and the Financial System

Alexander Hamilton, as the first Secretary of the Treasury, played a pivotal role in shaping the economic policies of the early United States. He believed in a strong central government that could effectively manage the nation's finances and promote economic growth. Hamilton's financial system included the establishment of a national bank, the assumption of state debts, and the promotion of manufacturing through protective tariffs.

The creation of the First Bank of the United States in 1791 provided a stable financial institution that could issue currency, regulate credit, and facilitate economic transactions. The bank played a crucial role in stabilizing the nation's economy and promoting investment and economic growth.

Hamilton's policies also included the assumption of state debts incurred during the Revolutionary War. By assuming these debts, the federal government established its creditworthiness and strengthened its financial position. This move helped to establish the United States as a reliable borrower and laid the foundation for future economic growth.

Furthermore, Hamilton advocated for protective tariffs to protect American industries from foreign competition. He believed that tariffs would encourage domestic manufacturing and promote economic self-sufficiency. Although these policies faced opposition from those who believed in free trade, they laid the groundwork for the development of a strong industrial base in the United States.

Thomas Jefferson and Agrarianism

Thomas Jefferson, as the third President of the United States, pursued a different economic vision based on agrarianism. He believed that the future of the nation lay in its agricultural sector and that independent farmers were the backbone of a democratic society.

Jefferson opposed the establishment of a national bank, viewing it as an unconstitutional concentration of power. He believed that a decentralized banking system, with state-chartered banks, would better serve the interests of the people and prevent the concentration of wealth in the hands of a few.

Jefferson also favored a strict interpretation of the Constitution, which limited the powers of the federal government. He believed that the federal government should have limited involvement in economic affairs and that individual states should have the freedom to pursue their own economic policies.

While Jefferson's agrarian vision had its merits, it faced challenges as the nation grew and industrialization became more prevalent. The United States experienced rapid population growth and urbanization, leading to increased demand for manufactured goods. Jefferson's emphasis on agriculture and his opposition to industrialization limited the nation's ability to compete in the global market and hindered its economic development.

The Legacy of Economic Policies

The economic policies of the Founding Fathers had a profound and lasting impact on the American economy. Hamilton's vision of a strong central government and a diversified economy laid the foundation for the nation's industrialization and economic growth. His financial system, including the establishment of a national bank and protective tariffs, provided stability and promoted investment.

Jefferson's agrarian vision, while rooted in the principles of independence and self-sufficiency, faced challenges as the nation evolved. The United States embraced industrialization and urbanization, leading to a shift away from an agrarian economy. However, Jefferson's emphasis on limited government intervention and individual freedoms continues to shape the American economic landscape.

The economic policies of the Founding Fathers set the stage for the United States to become a global economic powerhouse. Their debates and compromises laid the foundation for a mixed economy that combines elements of capitalism and government intervention. The legacy of their economic policies can be seen in the development of a strong financial system, a diverse industrial base, and a commitment to free trade.

As the United States continues to navigate economic challenges and opportunities, it is important to reflect on the economic principles and debates of the Founding Fathers. Their vision and policies continue to shape the American economy and provide valuable lessons for future generations.

The Founding Fathers and the Expansion of the Nation

10.1 Westward Expansion and Manifest Destiny

The concept of Westward Expansion and Manifest Destiny played a significant role in shaping the United States of America as we know it today. It was a period of territorial growth and exploration that spanned from the early 19th century to the mid-19th century. This chapter explores the motivations, challenges, and consequences of this expansionist movement.

The Idea of Manifest Destiny

Manifest Destiny was a belief that emerged in the 19th century, asserting that it was the destiny and duty of the United States to expand its territory from coast to coast. This idea was rooted in a combination of religious, economic, and political factors. Many Americans believed that it was their divine mission to spread democracy, Christianity, and American values across the continent.

Motivations for Westward Expansion

There were several motivations behind the push for Westward Expansion. One of the primary reasons was the desire for land and resources. As the population grew, there was a need for more space to accommodate the increasing number of settlers. Additionally, the discovery of valuable resources such as gold and silver in the West further fueled the desire for expansion.

Another motivation was the belief in the superiority of American culture and institutions. Many Americans saw themselves as the torchbearers of democracy and believed that their way of life should be extended to the entire continent. This sense of exceptionalism drove the push for expansion.

The Louisiana Purchase

One of the most significant events in Westward Expansion was the Louisiana Purchase in 1803. President Thomas Jefferson negotiated the purchase of a vast territory from France, doubling the size of the United States overnight. This acquisition opened up new opportunities for settlement and exploration, setting the stage for further expansion.

Lewis and Clark Expedition

In 1804, President Jefferson commissioned Meriwether Lewis and William Clark to lead an expedition to explore the newly acquired western territory. The Lewis and Clark Expedition, also known as the Corps of Discovery, aimed to map the land, establish trade with Native American tribes, and find a water route to the Pacific Ocean. Their journey was arduous and filled with challenges, but it provided valuable information about the geography, flora, fauna, and Native American tribes of the region.

The Oregon Trail and the California Gold Rush

The 1840s witnessed a surge in westward migration, primarily driven by the promise of fertile land and economic opportunities. The Oregon Trail became a popular route for pioneers seeking a better life in the fertile valleys of the Pacific Northwest. Simultaneously, the discovery of gold in California in 1848 sparked the famous California Gold Rush, attracting thousands of fortune seekers from all over the world.

The Mexican-American War

The Mexican-American War, fought between 1846 and 1848, was a significant event in Westward Expansion. The war was primarily driven by territorial disputes between the United States and Mexico, with the United States seeking to acquire vast territories in the Southwest, including present-day California, New Mexico, Arizona, Nevada, Utah, and parts of Colorado and Wyoming.

The United States emerged victorious, and the Treaty of Guadalupe Hidalgo in 1848 officially ceded these territories to the United States.

Consequences of Westward Expansion

Westward Expansion had profound consequences for both the United States and the Native American tribes who inhabited the land. While it led to the growth and development of the United States, it also resulted in the displacement, marginalization, and mistreatment of Native American communities. The forced removal of Native Americans from their ancestral lands, such as the Trail of Tears, remains a dark chapter in American history.

Additionally, Westward Expansion intensified tensions between the North and the South over the issue of slavery. The question of whether newly acquired territories would allow slavery or be free states became a central point of contention, ultimately leading to the American Civil War.

The Legacy of Territorial Expansion

The legacy of Westward Expansion and Manifest Destiny is still evident in the United States today. The acquisition of vast territories shaped the country's physical boundaries and laid the foundation for its economic and political power. It also contributed to the idea of American exceptionalism and the belief in the nation's destiny to lead and shape the world.

However, it is essential to recognize the human cost of this expansion. Native American communities suffered greatly, losing their lands, cultures, and lives in the process. The consequences of Westward Expansion continue to be felt and acknowledged as part of the ongoing efforts towards reconciliation and justice.

In conclusion, Westward Expansion and Manifest Destiny were defining chapters in American history. Motivated by a sense of destiny, economic opportunities, and a belief in American exceptionalism, the United States expanded its territory from coast to coast. This expansion had far-reaching consequences, both positive and negative, shaping the nation's identity and leaving a lasting impact on Native American communities.

10.2 Lewis and Clark Expedition

The Lewis and Clark Expedition, also known as the Corps of Discovery, was a landmark journey that played a crucial role in the expansion of the United States and the exploration of the American West. Led by Meriwether Lewis and William Clark, this expedition was commissioned by President Thomas Jefferson in 1803 with the primary objective of exploring and mapping the newly acquired Louisiana Purchase territory.

Background and Preparation

In 1803, President Jefferson saw the Louisiana Purchase as an opportunity to expand the young nation's borders and gain valuable knowledge about the vast western territories. To accomplish this, he selected Meriwether Lewis, his personal secretary, and William Clark, a skilled frontiersman and former army officer, to lead the expedition. Lewis and Clark were chosen for their leadership qualities, scientific knowledge, and familiarity with the western frontier.

The expedition was meticulously planned, with Jefferson providing detailed instructions to Lewis on what he hoped to achieve. The primary goals were to find a practical route to the Pacific Ocean, establish diplomatic relations with Native American tribes, document the flora and fauna of the region, and gather information about the geography, geology, and resources of the newly acquired territory.

The Journey Begins

On May 14, 1804, the Corps of Discovery set out from St. Louis, Missouri, in a keelboat and two smaller pirogues. The expedition consisted of a diverse group of approximately 40 men, including soldiers, interpreters, hunters, and boatmen. They traveled up the Missouri River, facing numerous challenges such as treacherous rapids, harsh weather conditions, and encounters with Native American tribes.

Lewis and Clark maintained detailed journals throughout the journey, recording their observations of the landscape, wildlife, and interactions with Native Americans. These journals provided valuable information about the geography and natural resources of the western territories and helped shape future exploration and settlement.

Native American Encounters

One of the primary objectives of the expedition was to establish peaceful relations with Native American tribes and gather information about their cultures and territories. The Corps of Discovery encountered numerous tribes along their route, including the Mandan, Hidatsa, Shoshone, Nez Perce, and many others.

Lewis and Clark relied on the services of Sacagawea, a Shoshone woman, and her husband Toussaint Charbonneau, as interpreters and guides. Sacagawea's presence proved invaluable, as her knowledge of the land and her ability to communicate with various tribes facilitated peaceful encounters and ensured the success of the expedition.

Challenges and Triumphs

The journey was not without its challenges. The Corps of Discovery faced harsh weather, difficult terrain, and limited food supplies. They encountered grizzly bears, venomous snakes, and other wildlife that posed threats to their safety. However, through perseverance, resourcefulness, and the assistance of Native American tribes, they overcame these obstacles.

One of the most significant triumphs of the expedition was the successful crossing of the Rocky Mountains. The Corps of Discovery navigated treacherous mountain passes, endured freezing temperatures, and faced the constant threat of starvation. Their determination and resilience allowed them to reach the Pacific Ocean in November 1805, at a place now known as Cape Disappointment in present-day Washington State.

Scientific Discoveries and Legacy

In addition to their exploration and mapping efforts, Lewis and Clark made significant scientific discoveries during their expedition. They documented hundreds of plant and animal species previously unknown to science, providing valuable insights into the natural history of the region. Their findings expanded the scientific knowledge of the time and laid the foundation for future scientific exploration in the American West.

The Lewis and Clark Expedition's legacy extends far beyond their immediate achievements. Their journey opened up new possibilities for westward expansion, paved the way for future explorations, and solidified the United States' claim to the western territories. The expedition also fostered diplomatic relations with Native American tribes, contributing to peaceful interactions and trade in the region.

Conclusion

The Lewis and Clark Expedition stands as a testament to the courage, curiosity, and determination of the Founding Fathers and their vision for the expansion of the United States. Through their exploration and scientific discoveries, Lewis and Clark played a vital role in shaping the nation's understanding of the American West. Their expedition remains an enduring symbol of American exploration and the spirit of adventure that defined the early years of the United States.

10.3 The Mexican-American War

The Mexican-American War, which took place from 1846 to 1848, was a significant event in the history of the United States. It was a conflict between the United States and Mexico over territorial disputes and the desire for westward expansion. The war had profound consequences for both nations and played a crucial role in shaping the future of the United States.

Background and Causes of the War

The origins of the Mexican-American War can be traced back to the annexation of Texas by the United States in 1845. Texas had declared independence from Mexico in 1836 and had been an independent republic for nearly a decade. However, Mexico still considered Texas as part of its territory and viewed the annexation as a violation of its sovereignty.

The annexation of Texas was a contentious issue in the United States, with debates over the expansion of slavery and the potential for war with Mexico. President James K. Polk, a strong advocate of westward expansion, saw the annexation of Texas as a way to fulfill the concept of Manifest Destiny, the belief that it was the destiny of the United States to expand its territory from coast to coast.

The Outbreak of War

Tensions between the United States and Mexico escalated when American troops under the command of General Zachary Taylor were sent to the disputed border region between Texas and Mexico. In April 1846, a clash occurred between Mexican and American forces, resulting in the death of American soldiers. President Polk used this incident as a justification to declare war on Mexico.

The Mexican-American War was marked by a series of military engagements, including the Battles of Palo Alto, Resaca de la Palma, Monterrey, and Buena Vista. The American forces, led by General Taylor and later by General

Winfield Scott, achieved several victories and advanced into Mexican territory.

Consequences of the War

The Mexican-American War had significant consequences for both the United States and Mexico. The Treaty of Guadalupe Hidalgo, signed in 1848, ended the war and resulted in Mexico ceding a vast amount of territory to the United States. This included present-day California, Nevada, Utah, Arizona, New Mexico, and parts of Colorado and Wyoming. The acquisition of this territory nearly doubled the size of the United States.

The war also had profound implications for the issue of slavery. The acquisition of new territories reignited the debate over whether slavery should be allowed in these regions. The Compromise of 1850, which aimed to settle the issue, included provisions such as the admission of California as a free state and the implementation of the Fugitive Slave Act. These measures temporarily eased tensions but ultimately failed to resolve the underlying conflict.

Legacy and Impact

The Mexican-American War had a lasting impact on the relationship between the United States and Mexico. It created a sense of resentment and mistrust that persisted for many years. The loss of territory was a significant blow to Mexico, and the war exacerbated existing social and political divisions within the country.

For the United States, the war solidified its position as a continental power and accelerated the process of westward expansion. The acquisition of new territories provided opportunities for settlement, economic growth, and the spread of American influence. However, it also intensified the debate over the expansion of slavery and contributed to the growing tensions that would eventually lead to the American Civil War.

The Mexican-American War also highlighted the importance of diplomacy and the need for peaceful resolutions to territorial disputes. It served as a lesson for future generations about the consequences of war and the complexities of international relations.

Conclusion

The Mexican-American War was a pivotal event in the history of the United States. It was a conflict driven by the desire for westward expansion and territorial acquisition. The war had profound consequences for both the United States and Mexico, shaping the future of both nations and leaving a lasting impact on the issue of slavery and the relationship between the two countries. The Mexican-American War serves as a reminder of the complexities and consequences of war and the importance of diplomacy in resolving conflicts.

10.4 The Legacy of Territorial Expansion

The Founding Fathers of the United States were not only architects of a new nation but also pioneers of territorial expansion. Their vision for America extended far beyond the original thirteen colonies, and they actively pursued the acquisition of new lands to fulfill their dreams of a vast and prosperous nation. The legacy of their territorial expansion efforts has had a profound impact on the development and identity of the United States.

One of the key drivers of territorial expansion was the concept of Manifest Destiny, which emerged in the 19th century. Manifest Destiny was the belief that it was the destiny of the United States to expand its territory from coast to coast, spreading democracy and civilization along the way. This ideology fueled the desire for westward expansion and the acquisition of new lands.

The Louisiana Purchase of 1803 stands as one of the most significant achievements in American territorial expansion. President Thomas Jefferson, a staunch advocate of westward expansion, negotiated the purchase of the vast Louisiana Territory from France. This acquisition doubled the size of the United States and opened up new opportunities for settlement and economic growth. The Louisiana Purchase paved the way for the exploration and colonization of the American West.

To explore and map the newly acquired territory, President Jefferson commissioned the famous Lewis and Clark Expedition. Led by Meriwether Lewis and William Clark, this expedition set out in 1804 to explore the western lands and find a route to the Pacific Ocean. Their journey was arduous and filled with challenges, but it provided valuable information about the geography, resources, and Native American tribes of the region. The Lewis and Clark Expedition played a crucial role in expanding American knowledge and influence in the West.

Another significant expansion of American territory came as a result of the Mexican-American War (1846-1848). The war was fought over territorial disputes between the United States and Mexico, with the United States ultimately emerging victorious. The Treaty of Guadalupe Hidalgo, signed in 1848, ended the war and ceded a vast amount of territory to the United States, including present-day California, Nevada, Utah, Arizona, New Mexico, and parts of Colorado and Wyoming. This acquisition further solidified America's presence in the West and set the stage for future expansion.

The legacy of territorial expansion is multifaceted and has had both positive and negative consequences. On the positive side, it allowed for the growth of the United States into a continental power. The acquisition of new lands provided opportunities for settlement, economic development, and the spread of American ideals and institutions. It also fueled the spirit of exploration and adventure that has become ingrained in the American identity.

However, territorial expansion also had its dark side. The acquisition of new lands often came at the expense of Native American tribes who were forcibly displaced from their ancestral lands. The expansionist policies of the United States led to conflicts and wars with Native American tribes, resulting in the loss of their lands, cultures, and lives. The legacy of this displacement and mistreatment continues to impact Native American communities to this day.

Territorial expansion also exacerbated tensions over the issue of slavery. The acquisition of new lands reignited the debate over whether these territories would allow slavery or be free. This ultimately led to the sectional divide that culminated in the American Civil War. The legacy of this division and the consequences of the war continue to shape American society and politics.

In conclusion, the Founding Fathers' pursuit of territorial expansion left a lasting legacy on the United States. Their vision for a vast and prosperous nation drove the acquisition of new lands and the exploration of the American West. While this expansion brought about economic growth and the spread of American ideals, it also resulted in the displacement of Native American tribes and intensified the debate over slavery. The legacy of territorial expansion continues to shape the United States, reminding us of the triumphs and consequences of the Founding Fathers' actions.

The Founding Fathers and the Formation of Political Parties

11.1 The Emergence of Political Factions

The formation of political parties in the United States can be traced back to the early years of the republic. As the new nation began to take shape, differing visions for its future emerged among the Founding Fathers. These differences in ideology and policy led to the emergence of political factions, which eventually evolved into the first political parties in American history.

The seeds of political division were sown during the debates over the ratification of the Constitution. Two main factions emerged during this period: the Federalists and the Anti-Federalists. The Federalists, led by Alexander Hamilton, James Madison, and John Adams, supported a strong central government and the ratification of the Constitution. They believed that a strong federal government was necessary to maintain order and protect the rights of the people. On the other hand, the Anti-Federalists, led by Thomas Jefferson and Patrick Henry, were skeptical of a strong central government and feared that it would infringe upon the rights of the states and individuals.

The Federalists and Anti-Federalists engaged in a spirited debate over the merits of the Constitution. The Federalists argued that a strong central government was necessary to address the weaknesses of the Articles of Confederation and ensure the stability and prosperity of the new nation. They believed that a strong executive branch, a bicameral legislature, and an independent judiciary were essential for effective governance. The Anti-Federalists, however, expressed concerns about the potential for tyranny and the lack of a Bill of Rights to protect individual liberties.

Despite their differences, both factions shared a common goal: the establishment of a stable and prosperous nation. They recognized the need for compromise and worked together to address the concerns of both sides. This spirit of compromise and cooperation laid the foundation for the formation of the first political parties in the United States.

The Federalist Party, which emerged in the 1790s, was led by Alexander Hamilton and John Adams. It advocated for a strong central government, a strong military, and a pro-business economic policy. The party attracted support from urban elites, merchants, and manufacturers who believed in a strong federal government's ability to promote economic growth and protect their interests.

On the other hand, the Democratic-Republican Party, led by Thomas Jefferson and James Madison, emerged as the main opposition to the Federalists. The Democratic-Republicans favored a more limited role for the federal government, emphasizing states' rights and agrarian interests. They believed in a strict interpretation of the Constitution and were skeptical of the powers of the central government.

The emergence of political parties had profound consequences for the young nation. It brought about a more organized and structured political system, with clear lines of ideological division. The parties served as vehicles for political mobilization and allowed citizens to align themselves with like-minded individuals. They also provided a platform for the expression of differing opinions and the competition of ideas.

However, the formation of political parties also led to increased polarization and partisanship. As the Federalists and Democratic-Republicans competed for power, political discourse became more divisive and acrimonious. Personal attacks and character assassinations became common, and the spirit of compromise that had characterized the early years of the republic began to erode.

Despite these challenges, the emergence of political factions played a crucial role in shaping the future of American democracy. It laid the groundwork for the development of a two-party system that has endured to this day. The Federalist Party eventually dissolved, but the Democratic-Republican Party evolved into the Democratic Party, which remains one of the two major political parties in the United States.

The formation of political parties also highlighted the importance of political engagement and citizen participation in a democratic society. It encouraged individuals to become informed about political issues, engage in political debates, and exercise their right to vote. The emergence of political factions served as a catalyst for the development of a vibrant and dynamic political culture in the United States.

In conclusion, the emergence of political factions among the Founding Fathers was a natural consequence of the differing visions for the future of the new nation. The Federalists and Anti-Federalists laid the foundation for the formation of the first political parties in the United States. While these factions brought about increased polarization and partisanship, they also played a crucial role in shaping the future of American democracy. The formation of political parties encouraged political engagement and citizen participation, laying the groundwork for the development of a two-party system that endures to this day.

11.2 Federalists vs. Anti-Federalists

The formation of political parties in the United States can be traced back to the early years of the nation's history. One of the most significant divisions among the Founding Fathers was the debate between the Federalists and the Anti-Federalists. This ideological clash played a crucial role in shaping the early political landscape of the United States and had far-reaching consequences for the future of the nation.

The Context of the Debate

The debate between the Federalists and the Anti-Federalists emerged during the ratification process of the United States Constitution. After the Constitutional Convention in 1787, the proposed Constitution needed to be ratified by at least nine of the thirteen states to become the supreme law of the land. However, this process was not without opposition.

The Anti-Federalists, a loose coalition of individuals who opposed the Constitution, argued that it granted too much power to the central government and threatened the rights of the states and individual liberties. They believed that a strong central government would inevitably lead to tyranny and the erosion of the hard-fought freedoms won during the Revolutionary War.

On the other hand, the Federalists, led by prominent figures such as Alexander Hamilton, James Madison, and John Jay, supported the Constitution and advocated for a stronger central government. They believed that a strong federal government was necessary to maintain order, protect the nation's interests, and ensure the success of the new republic.

The Federalist Papers

To sway public opinion in favor of the Constitution, the Federalists, particularly Hamilton, Madison, and Jay, wrote a series of essays known as the Federalist Papers. These essays, published between 1787 and 1788, provided a comprehensive defense of the Constitution and addressed the concerns raised by the Anti-Federalists.

The Federalist Papers presented a compelling argument for the necessity of a strong central government. They emphasized the importance of a balanced system of government, with separate branches that would check and balance each other's powers. The authors also highlighted the benefits of a unified nation, including a stronger defense against external threats and the ability to regulate commerce and trade.

Key Differences and Debates

The debate between the Federalists and the Anti-Federalists revolved around several key issues. One of the primary concerns of the Anti-Federalists was the absence of a Bill of Rights in the original Constitution. They argued that without explicit protections for individual liberties, the central government could easily infringe upon the rights of the people. This concern ultimately led to the inclusion of the Bill of Rights as the first ten amendments to the Constitution.

Another significant point of contention was the balance of power between the federal government and the states. The Anti-Federalists feared that a strong central government would undermine the authority of the states and diminish their ability to govern themselves. In contrast, the Federalists believed that a strong central government was necessary to prevent the disintegration of the nation and ensure uniformity in matters of national importance.

Compromises and Ratification

The debate between the Federalists and the Anti-Federalists was fierce and passionate. However, in the end, the Federalists were successful in securing the ratification of the Constitution. Their arguments, as presented in the Federalist Papers, resonated with many Americans who recognized the need for a strong and unified government.

To address the concerns of the Anti-Federalists, compromises were made. The promise of a Bill of Rights helped alleviate fears about the potential abuse of power by the federal government. Additionally, the Tenth Amendment, which reserved powers not delegated to the federal government to the states, provided some reassurance to those worried about the encroachment on state sovereignty.

Legacy and Impact

The debate between the Federalists and the Anti-Federalists had a lasting impact on the United States. It laid the foundation for the development of political parties and the ongoing struggle between the principles of federalism and states' rights. The Federalists' vision of a strong central government prevailed in the early years of the nation, shaping the course of American history.

The Federalist Papers, with their eloquent defense of the Constitution, continue to be studied and revered as a seminal work in American political thought. The debates between the Federalists and the Anti-Federalists also highlighted the importance of compromise and the ability to find common ground in the pursuit of a shared vision for the nation.

In conclusion, the clash between the Federalists and the Anti-Federalists during the ratification of the Constitution was a pivotal moment in American history. It represented a fundamental disagreement about the role and scope of the federal government and set the stage for the formation of political parties. The legacy of this debate continues to shape the political landscape of the United States to this day.

11.3 The Birth of the Democratic-Republican Party

The formation of political parties in the United States was a natural consequence of the differing visions and ideologies held by the Founding Fathers. While the Federalists and Anti-Federalists were the first major political factions to emerge, another significant party that played a crucial role in shaping the early American political landscape was the Democratic-Republican Party.

Origins and Ideology

The Democratic-Republican Party, also known as the Jeffersonian Republicans, was founded by Thomas Jefferson and James Madison in the early 1790s. It emerged as a response to the policies and actions of the Federalist Party, which was led by Alexander Hamilton and John Adams. The Democratic-Republicans believed in a strict interpretation of the Constitution, limited government power, and agrarianism.

One of the key ideological differences between the Federalists and the Democratic-Republicans was their stance on the role of the federal government. The Federalists advocated for a strong central government with broad powers, while the Democratic-Republicans favored a more decentralized system, with power residing primarily in the states. They believed that a strong central government could potentially infringe upon individual liberties and lead to the consolidation of power.

Opposition to Federalist Policies

The Democratic-Republican Party emerged as a vocal opposition to the Federalist Party's policies, particularly those championed by Alexander Hamilton. Hamilton's economic vision, which included a national bank, protective tariffs, and a strong industrial base, was seen by the Democratic-

Republicans as favoring the wealthy elite and neglecting the interests of the common people, especially farmers.

Jefferson and Madison, the primary architects of the Democratic-Republican Party, sought to promote an agrarian society and protect the rights of farmers. They believed that the strength of the nation lay in its agricultural sector and that the government should support and protect the interests of farmers through policies such as low tariffs and limited government intervention in the economy.

The Election of 1800

The election of 1800 marked a significant turning point in American politics and solidified the Democratic-Republican Party's position as a major political force. The election was a bitter contest between Thomas Jefferson and the incumbent president, John Adams, who was a Federalist. The campaign was characterized by intense political rhetoric and personal attacks.

Jefferson's victory in the election was seen as a triumph for the Democratic-Republican Party and a repudiation of Federalist policies. It was the first time in American history that power was peacefully transferred from one political party to another. The election demonstrated the strength and popularity of the Democratic-Republicans, who were able to mobilize support from a broad range of voters, including farmers, artisans, and urban workers.

Jefferson's Presidency

Thomas Jefferson's presidency, which lasted from 1801 to 1809, was marked by his commitment to the principles of the Democratic-Republican Party. He sought to limit the power of the federal government, reduce the national debt, and promote agrarian interests. One of his most significant achievements was the Louisiana Purchase in 1803, which doubled the size of the United States and opened up vast new territories for westward expansion.

During his presidency, Jefferson also faced challenges such as the conflict with the Barbary pirates in North Africa and the embargo imposed on American trade with foreign nations. These challenges tested the effectiveness of his policies and the ability of the Democratic-Republican Party to govern effectively.

Legacy and Evolution

The Democratic-Republican Party played a crucial role in shaping the early American political landscape and laying the foundation for the two-party system that continues to this day. While the party eventually dissolved in the 1820s, its legacy endured through the principles and ideas it championed.

The Democratic-Republican Party's emphasis on limited government, states' rights, and agrarianism influenced subsequent political movements and parties. It provided a counterbalance to the Federalist Party's vision of a strong central government and helped shape the ongoing debate over the balance of power between the federal government and the states.

The party's commitment to individual liberties and a strict interpretation of the Constitution also left a lasting impact on American political thought. These principles continue to be invoked and debated by politicians and scholars alike, as they grapple with the challenges of governing in a democratic society.

In conclusion, the birth of the Democratic-Republican Party marked a significant moment in American history. It represented a distinct ideological alternative to the Federalist Party and played a crucial role in shaping the early American political landscape. The party's commitment to limited government, agrarianism, and states' rights left a lasting impact on American political thought and helped shape the ongoing debate over the role of government in society.

11.4 The Evolution of American Political Parties

The formation of political parties in the United States was not something that the Founding Fathers initially anticipated or desired. In fact, many of them warned against the dangers of factionalism and the potential for parties to divide the nation. However, despite their concerns, political parties began to emerge shortly after the ratification of the Constitution, and they have played a significant role in shaping American politics ever since.

Early Political Factions

The first political factions in the United States can be traced back to the debates over the ratification of the Constitution. Those who supported the ratification, known as Federalists, believed in a strong central government and were led by prominent figures such as Alexander Hamilton and John Adams. On the other side were the Anti-Federalists, who opposed the Constitution because they feared it would concentrate too much power in the hands of the federal government. Anti-Federalists, including Thomas Jefferson and Patrick Henry, argued for greater state sovereignty and individual liberties.

Federalists vs. Democratic-Republicans

The divide between Federalists and Anti-Federalists laid the foundation for the first major political parties in the United States. After the ratification of the Constitution, the Federalist Party emerged as the dominant political force. They advocated for a strong federal government, a national bank, and close ties with Britain. However, their policies and elitist tendencies led to growing opposition.

In response to the Federalists, Thomas Jefferson and James Madison formed the Democratic-Republican Party, also known as the Jeffersonian Republicans. They believed in limited government, agrarianism, and a strict interpretation of the Constitution. The Democratic-Republicans gained support from farmers, artisans, and those who felt marginalized by the Federalist establishment.

The Era of Good Feelings and the Rise of the Democrats

Following the War of 1812, the Federalist Party began to decline, and the United States entered a period known as the Era of Good Feelings. During this time, there was a sense of national unity and a lack of significant political opposition. However, this era was short-lived, and new political divisions soon emerged.

In the 1820s, the Democratic-Republican Party split into two factions: the National Republicans, led by John Quincy Adams and Henry Clay, and the Democratic Party, led by Andrew Jackson. The National Republicans advocated for a strong federal government and supported policies such as protective tariffs and internal improvements. The Democratic Party, on the other hand, championed states' rights, limited government, and the interests of the common man.

The Whigs and the Second Party System

By the 1830s, the Democratic Party, under the leadership of Andrew Jackson, had become the dominant political force in the United States. However, opposition to Jackson's policies and his use of executive power led to the formation of a new political party, the Whigs.

The Whig Party, which included former National Republicans and Anti-Jackson Democrats, emerged as the main opposition to the Democrats. They advocated for a strong federal government, internal improvements, and a protective tariff. The Whigs also sought to limit the power of the presidency and promote a more active role for Congress.

The rivalry between the Democrats and the Whigs marked the beginning of the Second Party System in the United States. This system was characterized by intense competition between the two major parties, with elections often turning on issues such as slavery, economic policies, and the balance of power between the federal government and the states.

The Birth of the Republican Party

The Second Party System began to unravel in the 1850s, primarily due to the issue of slavery. As tensions between the North and the South escalated, a new political party emerged: the Republican Party. The Republican Party was founded in 1854 by anti-slavery activists, former Whigs, and members of the Free Soil Party.

The Republican Party's primary goal was to prevent the spread of slavery into new territories. They believed in the principles of free labor, economic development, and the preservation of the Union. In 1860, the Republican Party nominated Abraham Lincoln as its presidential candidate, and he went on to win the election, leading to the secession of several Southern states and the outbreak of the Civil War.

The Modern Era of Political Parties

Following the Civil War, the Republican Party emerged as the dominant political force in the United States. They championed policies such as industrialization, economic growth, and westward expansion. However, the Democratic Party remained a significant opposition force, particularly in the South.

Throughout the 20th century, the two major parties continued to evolve and adapt to the changing political landscape. The Democratic Party shifted its focus to issues such as civil rights, social welfare, and labor rights, while the Republican Party embraced conservative principles, limited government, and free-market economics.

In recent decades, third-party movements and independent candidates have also played a role in American politics, challenging the dominance of the two major parties. However, the Republican and Democratic parties have remained the primary vehicles for political power and continue to shape the direction of the nation.

Conclusion

The evolution of American political parties has been a complex and dynamic process. From the early divisions between Federalists and Anti-Federalists to the emergence of the Democratic and Republican parties, political factions have played a crucial role in shaping the course of American history.

While the Founding Fathers may have warned against the dangers of political parties, they ultimately laid the groundwork for their formation through their own disagreements and debates. The evolution of political parties reflects the ongoing struggle to balance competing interests and ideologies within a democratic system.

As the United States continues to grapple with new challenges and debates, the legacy of the Founding Fathers and the evolution of political parties serve as a reminder of the ongoing quest for a more perfect union.

The Founding Fathers

12.1 The Enduring Influence of the Founding Fathers

The Founding Fathers of the United States of America were a remarkable group of individuals who played a pivotal role in shaping the nation's history. Their enduring influence can be seen in the principles and ideals that continue to guide the country to this day. From the architects of the Declaration of Independence to the framers of the Constitution, their victories, triumphs, and consequences have created the greatest nation in history.

The Founding Fathers were driven by a shared vision of a nation founded on the principles of liberty, equality, and justice. They believed in the inherent rights of individuals and the importance of limited government. Through their collective efforts, they established a system of government that would serve as a model for democracies around the world.

One of the most significant triumphs of the Founding Fathers was the drafting and adoption of the Declaration of Independence. This document, written primarily by Thomas Jefferson, proclaimed the colonies' independence from British rule and laid out the fundamental principles upon which the new nation would be built. The Declaration declared that all men are created equal and endowed with certain unalienable rights, including life, liberty, and the pursuit of happiness. This revolutionary idea would serve as the foundation for the American experiment in self-government.

Another triumph of the Founding Fathers was the creation of the Constitution of the United States. This remarkable document, drafted during the Constitutional Convention in 1787, established the framework for the American government. It outlined the powers and responsibilities of the three branches of government – the executive, legislative, and judicial – and provided a system of checks and balances to prevent the abuse of power. The Constitution also included a Bill of Rights, which guaranteed certain individual liberties and protections.

The consequences of the Founding Fathers' actions were far-reaching and continue to shape the nation today. Their commitment to the principles of liberty and equality laid the groundwork for the abolition of slavery, the expansion of civil rights, and the ongoing struggle for social justice. The Founding Fathers' belief in the importance of a strong central government has guided the nation through times of crisis and allowed for the growth and development of the United States into a global superpower.

The enduring influence of the Founding Fathers can be seen in the interpretation and application of the Constitution. Their original intent and the principles they espoused continue to be debated and analyzed by scholars, jurists, and politicians. The Constitution is a living document, capable of adapting to the changing needs and values of society, thanks to the foresight and wisdom of the Founding Fathers.

The Founding Fathers' influence extends beyond the realm of politics and government. They have become iconic figures in American popular culture, revered for their wisdom, courage, and vision. Their names – George Washington, Thomas Jefferson, Benjamin Franklin, James Madison, and others – are synonymous with the birth of the nation and the ideals it represents. Their faces adorn currency, their statues stand in public squares, and their words are quoted in speeches and writings.

The lessons we can learn from the Founding Fathers are numerous. Their commitment to the principles of liberty, equality, and justice serves as a reminder of the importance of upholding these values in our own lives and in our society. They demonstrated the power of collaboration and compromise, showing that even in the face of differing opinions and interests, it is possible to find common ground and work towards a shared goal. The Founding Fathers also remind us of the importance of civic engagement and active participation in the democratic process. They understood that the success of the nation depended on the informed and active involvement of its citizens.

In conclusion, the Founding Fathers were extraordinary individuals who left an indelible mark on the history of the United States. Their victories, triumphs, and consequences created a nation founded on the principles of liberty, equality, and justice. Their enduring influence can be seen in the Constitution, the interpretation of its principles, and the ongoing pursuit of the ideals they championed. The Founding Fathers continue to inspire and guide us as we strive to build a more perfect union.

12.2 Interpreting the Constitution

The United States Constitution is the supreme law of the land, serving as the foundation for the American government and the rights and freedoms of its citizens. As the architects of this remarkable document, the Founding Fathers left behind a legacy that continues to shape the nation to this day. However, interpreting the Constitution has been a subject of debate and controversy throughout American history.

The Constitution was written in 1787 during the Constitutional Convention in Philadelphia. Its purpose was to establish a framework for the new government and to address the weaknesses of the Articles of Confederation. The Founding Fathers, with their diverse backgrounds and perspectives, worked together to create a document that would balance power between the federal government and the states, while also protecting individual rights.

One of the key challenges in interpreting the Constitution lies in its brevity. The document consists of only seven articles and twenty-seven amendments, leaving many important issues open to interpretation. The Founding Fathers intentionally crafted the Constitution to be flexible and adaptable to the changing needs of the nation. However, this flexibility has also led to differing interpretations of its provisions.

The first major debate in interpreting the Constitution arose between the Federalists and the Anti-Federalists. The Federalists, led by Alexander Hamilton, believed in a broad interpretation of the Constitution, arguing for a strong central government. On the other hand, the Anti-Federalists, led by Thomas Jefferson, advocated for a strict interpretation, emphasizing the rights of the states and individual liberties. This debate laid the foundation for the ongoing tension between federal and state powers.

One of the most significant challenges in interpreting the Constitution is determining the original intent of the Founding Fathers. Some argue that the Constitution should be interpreted based on the original meaning of its words and phrases at the time it was written. This approach, known as originalism, seeks to understand the intentions of the Founding Fathers and apply them to modern-day issues. Others believe in a more flexible approach, known as living constitutionalism, which takes into account the evolving societal and cultural context.

The Supreme Court plays a crucial role in interpreting the Constitution. Through landmark cases, the Court has shaped the interpretation of various constitutional provisions. For example, in Marbury v. Madison (1803), the Court established the power of judicial review, allowing it to declare laws unconstitutional. This decision solidified the Court's authority in interpreting the Constitution and has had a lasting impact on American jurisprudence.

Over the years, the interpretation of the Constitution has been at the center of many significant legal and political debates. Issues such as civil rights, the scope of presidential power, and the balance between individual liberties and national security have all been subject to interpretation. Different justices and legal scholars have offered varying perspectives, leading to a rich and ongoing dialogue about the meaning and application of the Constitution.

Interpreting the Constitution is not limited to the legal realm. It also extends to the realm of public opinion and political discourse. Political leaders and citizens alike often invoke the Constitution to support their positions on various issues. This has led to a vibrant and sometimes contentious public debate about the proper interpretation of the Constitution and its relevance to contemporary society.

The Founding Fathers could not have anticipated all the challenges and complexities that would arise in interpreting the Constitution. However, they understood the importance of creating a document that could withstand the test of time. They recognized that the Constitution would need to be interpreted and adapted to the changing needs and values of future generations.

In conclusion, interpreting the Constitution is an ongoing and dynamic process. The Founding Fathers left behind a remarkable document that continues to guide the nation, but its interpretation is subject to differing perspectives and evolving societal norms. The debates and discussions surrounding the interpretation of the Constitution reflect the enduring relevance and importance of the Founding Fathers' vision for a democratic and free society.

12.3 The Founders in Popular Culture

The Founding Fathers of the United States have left an indelible mark on American history and continue to be revered as the architects of the nation. Their contributions to the birth of the United States and the formation of its government have been widely celebrated and studied. Over the years, the Founding Fathers have also become prominent figures in popular culture, appearing in various forms of media, including books, films, television shows, and even musicals. Their portrayal in popular culture has both shaped and been shaped by public perception and understanding of these historical figures.

One of the most well-known portrayals of the Founding Fathers in popular culture is the Broadway musical "Hamilton," created by Lin-Manuel Miranda. The musical tells the story of Alexander Hamilton, one of the Founding Fathers, through a blend of hip-hop, R&B, and traditional show tunes. "Hamilton" not only brings the Founding Fathers to life on stage but also reimagines their stories and personalities in a contemporary and diverse context. The musical's popularity has sparked a renewed interest in the Founding Fathers and has introduced their stories to a new generation.

In addition to "Hamilton," numerous films and television shows have depicted the lives and achievements of the Founding Fathers. One notable example is the HBO miniseries "John Adams," based on the biography by David McCullough. The series provides a detailed and historically accurate portrayal of John Adams, the second President of the United States and one of the key figures in the American Revolution. Through its meticulous attention to historical detail, "John Adams" offers viewers a glimpse into the challenges and triumphs faced by the Founding Fathers.

Popular culture has also explored the personal lives and relationships of the Founding Fathers. The 2008 HBO miniseries "John Adams" delves into the complex relationship between John Adams and his wife, Abigail Adams, highlighting her influence on his political career. Similarly, the 1995 film

"Jefferson in Paris" explores the romantic relationship between Thomas Jefferson and his slave, Sally Hemings. These portrayals humanize the Founding Fathers, showcasing their flaws, vulnerabilities, and personal struggles.

The Founding Fathers have also been the subject of numerous biographies and historical novels. These works of fiction often provide a more intimate and imaginative portrayal of the Founding Fathers, delving into their thoughts, emotions, and motivations. Novels such as "1776" by David McCullough and "Burr" by Gore Vidal offer readers a fictionalized account of the events surrounding the American Revolution and the early years of the United States. These works not only entertain but also provide readers with a deeper understanding of the complexities and contradictions of the Founding Fathers.

Beyond books and films, the Founding Fathers have made their way into popular culture through various symbols and iconography. The faces of George Washington, Thomas Jefferson, Benjamin Franklin, and other Founding Fathers adorn U.S. currency, stamps, and monuments. Their words and ideas are often quoted in political speeches and used as inspiration for patriotic songs. The Founding Fathers have become enduring symbols of American ideals such as liberty, democracy, and individual rights.

However, it is important to note that popular culture often simplifies and romanticizes the lives of the Founding Fathers. The complexities and contradictions of their beliefs and actions are often overlooked or glossed over. For example, the issue of slavery, which was deeply intertwined with the lives of many Founding Fathers, is often downplayed or ignored in popular portrayals. It is crucial to approach these depictions with a critical eye and seek a more nuanced understanding of the historical context in which the Founding Fathers lived.

In conclusion, the Founding Fathers have become prominent figures in popular culture, appearing in various forms of media and shaping public perception of their lives and achievements. From the Broadway musical "Hamilton" to historical novels and films, the Founding Fathers continue to captivate audiences and inspire a deeper appreciation for the history of the United States. However, it is important to recognize that popular portrayals often simplify and romanticize their stories, and a more nuanced understanding of their lives and legacies is necessary to fully grasp their contributions to the nation.

12.4 Lessons from the Founding Fathers

The Founding Fathers of the United States were not only architects of a new nation but also visionaries who laid the foundation for a democratic society. Their triumphs and consequences have shaped the course of American history and continue to influence the nation today. As we reflect on their legacy, there are valuable lessons we can learn from these remarkable individuals.

1. The Importance of Unity and Compromise

One of the most significant lessons we can learn from the Founding Fathers is the importance of unity and compromise. Despite their diverse backgrounds, beliefs, and interests, they recognized the necessity of working together for the greater good. The Constitutional Convention itself was a testament to their ability to find common ground and reach compromises that would benefit the entire nation. This lesson reminds us that progress can only be achieved through collaboration and a willingness to set aside personal differences for the sake of the collective.

2. The Power of Vision and Ideals

The Founding Fathers were driven by a powerful vision of a nation founded on principles of liberty, equality, and justice. Their ideals continue to inspire generations of Americans and serve as a reminder of the values that define the nation. Their unwavering commitment to these principles teaches us the importance of having a clear vision and staying true to our ideals, even in the face of adversity.

3. The Need for Constant Vigilance

The Founding Fathers understood that the preservation of liberty and democracy required constant vigilance. They recognized that the power of government must be limited and that the rights of individuals must be protected. This lesson reminds us that we must remain vigilant in safeguarding our democratic institutions and ensuring that the principles upon which our nation was founded are upheld.

4. The Value of Civic Engagement

The Founding Fathers believed in the power of an engaged citizenry. They understood that a thriving democracy requires active participation from its citizens. This lesson teaches us the importance of being informed, voting, and actively engaging in our communities. By taking an active role in shaping our society, we can honor the legacy of the Founding Fathers and contribute to the continued success of our nation.

5. The Imperfection of Human Nature

The Founding Fathers were well aware of the imperfections of human nature. They understood that power could corrupt and that individuals were prone to selfishness and ambition. This awareness led them to design a system of checks and balances to prevent the concentration of power and protect against abuses. This lesson reminds us of the need for accountability and the importance of holding our leaders to high ethical standards.

6. The Value of Intellectual Discourse

The Founding Fathers engaged in rigorous intellectual discourse and debate. They understood the importance of considering different perspectives and challenging ideas. This lesson teaches us the value of open and respectful dialogue, even when we disagree. By engaging in thoughtful discourse, we can foster understanding, find common ground, and arrive at better solutions for the challenges we face as a nation.

7. The Legacy of Progress and Change

The Founding Fathers laid the groundwork for a nation that could adapt and evolve with the changing times. They understood that progress was necessary for the growth and prosperity of the nation. This lesson reminds us that change is inevitable and that we must be willing to embrace it while staying true to our core values. By learning from the past and embracing progress, we can continue to build upon the foundation laid by the Founding Fathers.

8. The Importance of Education

The Founding Fathers believed in the power of education to cultivate an informed and engaged citizenry. They recognized that an educated populace was essential for the success of a democratic society. This lesson teaches us the importance of investing in education and promoting lifelong learning. By empowering individuals with knowledge, we can ensure the continued vitality of our democracy.

9. The Courage to Challenge the Status Quo

The Founding Fathers demonstrated immense courage in challenging the status quo and fighting for their vision of a new nation. They were willing to risk their lives, fortunes, and reputations for the cause of liberty. This lesson reminds us of the importance of courage and the need to challenge injustice and inequality. By standing up for what is right, we can create a more just and equitable society.

10. The Legacy of Hope and Inspiration

Perhaps the most enduring lesson from the Founding Fathers is the legacy of hope and inspiration they have left behind. Their belief in the potential of the American experiment continues to inspire generations of Americans. This lesson teaches us the power of hope and the importance of believing in the possibility of a better future. By embracing the spirit of hope and optimism, we can continue to build upon the foundation laid by the Founding Fathers and create a brighter tomorrow.

In conclusion, the Founding Fathers of the United States were not only architects of a new nation but also visionaries who left behind a lasting legacy.

Their triumphs and consequences have shaped the course of American history and continue to influence the nation today. By learning from their lessons of unity, compromise, vision, and civic engagement, we can honor their legacy and contribute to the ongoing success of our great nation.